Singapore's
BUSINESS PARK
REAL ESTATE

- Viability, Design & Planning of the Knowledge-Based
Urban Development (KBUD)

Kim Hin David HO

PARTRIDGE

To order additional copies of this book, contact
Toll Free +65 3165 7531 (Singapore)
Toll Free +60 3 3099 4412 (Malaysia)
orders.singapore@partridgepublishing.com

www.partridgepublishing.com/singapore

Contents

Foreword

"Over 100 years ago, this (Singapore) was a mud-flat,
swamp. Today, this is a modern city. Ten years from
now, this will be a metropolis. Never fear."

(The first Prime Minister of Singapore
Lee Kuan Yew, 1965)

This book highlights and discusses the viability, design and planning
of the large -scale high-tech strategic business park real estate asset class
in Singapore, with respect to the knowledge based urban development
(KBUD). Chapter 1 looks at the behavioral structure of the large and
strategic industrial real estate accommodation, which does not exist in a
vacuum. The fundamental investment values and yields of the large and
strategic industrial real estate accommodation, are uniquely affected
via the dynamic interaction between exogenous and endogenous
forces, relating to industrial real estate demand-supply conditions,
macroeconomic conditions and institutional polices. Chapter 1 seeks
to understand the dynamic behavior of industrial real estate market
in Singapore, which is gradually transitioning from a capital intensive
to a more knowledge intensive economy. Data is available for research
purposes from 2001Q4 to 2010Q4 that is long enough to capture three
property cycles.

Chapter 2 looks discusses a rigorous econometric model estimation,
adopting a vector auto regressive (VAR) approach to understand

the relationship between the overall industrial net space absorption, vacancy rate, capitalization rates and property price indices, to other macroeconomic variables. The required data set is historical and readily available for research purposes with respect to relevant factors, affecting the behavioral structure of strategic industrial real estate from 2000Q4 to 2010Q4. The data set is obtained via authoritative local government agencies like the URA (urban redevelopment authority) and the JTC (Jurong town corporation), international data sources. Secondary private online data agencies include DATASTREAM and Singapore's Real Estate Information System (REALIS), which offer a clear understanding of the dynamic behavior, which is exhibited by the strategic industrial real estate market in Singapore. Chapter 2 seeks to understand the interrelationships between strategic industrial real estate and macroeconomic variables, via impulse response and the variance decomposition analyses under the VAR model.

Chapter 3 proposes the knowledge interaction design criteria (KIDC) to enable urban planners to associate the related actors in space. With such a KIDC, the important rationale is satisfied when performing land use zoning, to integrate compatible land uses, which generate positive externalities so that they are mutually beneficial. Chapter 3 offers a formal representation of the knowledge based urban development-land use design model (KBUD-LUDM), incorporating the KI interaction design criteria, the KDIC via adopting agent-based modelling (ABM), to obtain the optimal land use design solutions. Chapter 3 discusses how to identify and classify the complementary actors (i.e. the group) in a planned post-industrial KBUD. Chapter 3 also offers a dynamic alternative planning approach to 'zone' the KBUD via the agent-based model (ABM).

Chapter 4 is concerned with several essential contributions to the design and planning literature of post-industrial clusters. Chapter 4 also discusses the simulation results and findings of the 'Knowledge-Based Urban Development-Land Use Design Model' (KBUD-LUDM), utilizing Singapore's Biopolis at the One North knowledge-based urban development (KBUD). Chapter 4 offers the basic assumptions of the KBUD-LUDM that are required to initialize and conduct the subsequent scenario analysis. The Chapter deals with the 'Baseline Scenario' simulation for the Biopolis One North KBUD, while such a simulation model's agent initialization procedure (AIP) is estimated from surveys and interviews.

In effect, the Baseline Scenario is used as a benchmark to project scenarios of plausible future states of the Biopolis at One North KBUD. Chapter 4 demonstrates the KBUD-LUDM's flexibility in performing incremental planning because land-use demand fluctuates over time. Chapter 4 therefore looks into the required validation and visualization procedures. Chapter 4 brings due attention to the entire study, its questions, approach, results and findings. Several directions for extending the KBUD-LUDM via the inclusion of multiple design criteria, for the comprehensive multi-dimensional land-use design modelling, are discussed.

Chapter 5 concludes this book.

Happy reading.

Yours sincerely,
Professor (Dr) HO, Kim Hin / David
Singapore
October 2021.

Acknowledgements

The Author wishes to extend his most sincere appreciation to the School of Design & Environment, under the highly able Deanship of the Provost & Chair Professor (Dr) LAM Khee Poh, of the National University of Singapore. The same wish is extended to the University of Cambridge and the University of Hertfordshire in Hatfield, UK. These three tertiary institutions of higher learning and research are globally leading Universities, inspiring and encouraging both modern and contemporary studies of large and complex physical infrastructural provision, in particularly the large-scale high-tech strategic direct real estate developments.

About The Author

Professor (Dr) HO, Kim Hin / David

PhD (Development Economics) (Cambridge), MPhil (1st Cl Hons and a Star for Distinction) (Development Studies & Land Economy) (Cambridge); Honorary Professor (Development Economics & Land Economy) (Uni of Hertfordshire); Honorary Doctorate of Letters (International Biographical Centre) (Cambridge); Systems Engineering (US Naval Postgraduate School), MRES (UK), AM NCREIF (US), FARES (US), MAEA (US), MESS, MSIM. Retired Professor (Associate) (Tenured) (International Real Estate) (Department of Real Estate) (School of Design and Environment) (National University of Singapore, NUS). Home Address: Block 220 Ang Mo Kio Avenue 1 #02-807, Singapore 560220; email address: davidhokh1@gmail.com.

Professor HO Kim Hin / David spent 31 years across several sectors, including the military, oil refining, aerospace engineering, public housing, resettlement, land acquisition, reclamation and international real estate investing. 6 years were in Pidemco Land Ltd (now CapitaLand Ltd) and GIC Real Estate Pte Ltd. 17 years were in the NUS School of Design and Environment at the Department of Real Estate. He holds the Master of Philosophy (First Class Honours with Distinction), Doctor of Philosophy from the University of Cambridge; and the Honorary Professor from the University of Hertfordshire. He has published widely in 275 articles (inclusive of 91 articles in top peer reviewed, international journals; pertaining to real estate investment, real estate development, urban policy, consultancies, public cum private funded research projects and so also published 15 major books. He was governor of the St Gabriel's Foundation and member (District Judge equivalent) of the Valuation Review Board under the Singapore Ministry of Finance and the Singapore Courts.

The Introduction

The Design and Planning of the Knowledge Based Urban Development (KBUD) - Agent Based Modelling

This book reiterates that while cities remain essential geographical centres, it is imperative that knowledge is produced, marketed and exchanged locally. To design and plan the knowledge-based society, the 21st century city planners of the Organisation for Economic Cooperation and Development (OECD) suggest localised cluster-based initiatives, to stimulate innovation-based growth. Such clusters are construed to be the key industrial policy option, to sustain regional competitiveness and economic prosperity. Industrialised nations have developed large-scale regional- and metropolitan- level master plans, to design and plan the 'Knowledge-Based Urban Developments' (KBUDs). This book focuses on the urban planning and design aspects of such large-scale high-tech and strategic direct real estate developments, via adopting an agent-based modelling approach. Two key issues are highlighted for Singapore's 'One North'[1] Knowledge-Based Urban Development (KBUD), relating to land-use planning of mixed-use post-industrial cluster developments:

---

1   'One North' is a 200-hectare planned mixed-use development, conceived by the Singapore National Technology Plan 1991. One North is developed and launched in 2001 by the nation's industrial master planner, the JTC (Jurong Town Corporation).

1) First, stringent long-term urban plans and designs stipulated in traditional master plans have become inefficient tools, to guide development, because they are constantly subjected to changing market forces.

2) Secondly, land-use design objectives that seek to foster an 'interactive' environment remain sketchy, for large-scale Knowledge-Based Urban Developments (KBUDs), owing to the lack of underlying scientific principles to effectively guide them.

From theoretical insights of proximity dynamics, which focuses on the determinants of interactive learning, 'actors' are identified, and they participate in such KBUDs. Such actors are classified, based on their interaction needs with other agents. Under such a classification, a potential Knowledge Interaction Design Criteria (KIDC) is proposed and with the primary aim of enhancing 'knowledge interactions', among different 'actors' in the KBUDs. This book introduces a generic agent-based land-use design model, the 'Knowledge Based Urban Development-Land Use Design Model' (KBUD-LUDM). Such a KBUD-LUDM overcomes the shortcomings of the static master planning via the dynamic mixed usage of land uses for large-scale agent-based KBUDs. The KBUD-LUDM is driven by data from Singapore's Biopolis at the One North[2] KBUD. Such a KBUD plays a crucial role in reviving post-industrial cities in a twofold manner:

- Knowledge Interaction Design Criteria (KIDC) seeks to facilitate and enhance the intra-cluster interaction of post-industrial developments.
- An alternative dynamic planning tool, the KBUD-LUDM, to demonstrate an incremental planning approach, as compared to earlier land-use design models in the planning literature.

---

2   'One North' is about a 200-hectare planned mixed-use development, conceived by the Singapore National Technology Plan 1991. The Biopolis at the One North KBUD is developed and launched in 2001 by the state's industrial master planner, JTC (Jurong Town Corporation).

Future work can look at developing multiple design modules (or criteria) to extend the KBUD-LUDM's applicability. Several implications on current land-use design practices of post-industrial spaces, can be discussed.

Chapter 1 recognizes that Industrialized nations are undergoing a gradual shift of industrial policies, favoring a more knowledge intensive economy which in effect has created sustainable real estate demand for modern hi-tech industrial accommodation. Such modern hi-tech and specialized industrial real estate market is being constantly shaped by the institutional framework, market forces and other government policies. There is an apparent lack of understanding on how the institutional framework, vis-à-vis its interaction with macroeconomic conditions, can well affect the financial sustainability of a knowledge-based direct real estate development. Chapter 1 looks at the role of public institutions and market forces that shape the value of large-scale hi-tech strategic industrial accommodation. An in-depth and case-based investigation is undertaken of Singapore's Biopolis at One North, a large-scale high-tech strategic and integrated real estate development in Singapore. The Biopolis at One North is designed to be an iconic and intellectually stimulating environment for knowledge-based workers. Chapter 1 chronologically describes the role of the state of shaping the demand and investment potential of the large-scale high-tech strategic industrial spaces in Singapore. Utilizing macroeconomic and project level data, Chapter 1 evaluates the investment potential of Singapore's Biopolis at One North, via standard capital budgeting techniques and the multivariate copula risk analysis. The investment analysis of the Biopolis at One North suggests that under certain favorable macroeconomic conditions, such large-scale high-tech, strategic and specialized industrial real estate is gaining prominence among direct real estate developers, owing to this industrial real estate's attractiveness as a vital portfolio investment vehicle.

Chapter 2 reiterates that the behavioural structure of the large and strategic industrial real estate accommodation does not exist in a vacuum.

Its fundamental investment values and yields are uniquely affected through the dynamic interaction among exogenous and endogenous forces, relating to the industrial real estate demand-supply conditions, macroeconomic conditions and institutional polices. Chapter 2 seeks to understand the dynamic behaviour of the strategic industrial real estate market in Singapore that is slowly transitioning from a capital intensive to a more knowledge intensive economy. Using historical and readily available data from 2001Q4-2010Q4, which captures three property cycles, we incorporate a vector autoregressive (VAR) approach to holistically model the industrial real estate market with respect to its demand-supply conditions that capture the asset and space market behaviour. Chapter 2 helps policy makers and developers to understand the structure of Singapore's industrial real estate market with respect to its macroeconomic conditions. The results are insightful because they capture the public and private markets, along with the new hi-tech industrial accommodation, which is slowly gaining prominence at the turn of the 21st century, while Singapore strives towards a knowledge-based industrial economy.

Chapter 3 emphasizes that modern city planners have proposed localised cluster-based initiatives to spur innovative growth. Such industrial policies are integral to sustain regional competitiveness and prosperity. Large regional- and metropolitan- level master plans are undertaken to develop 'Knowledge-Based Urban Developments' (KBUDs). Chapter 3 focuses on the KBUD's design via agent-based modelling. Traditional land use master planning of the mixed use, post-industrial cluster developments are inefficient for KBUDs, subject to changing market forces. Land use objectives promote an 'interactive' physical environment, but they remain sketchy for large KBUDs. Chapter 3 discusses the KBUD 'actors' and classifies them, based on their interaction needs with other agents. A potential 'Knowledge Interaction Design Criteria' (KIDC) is introduced with the aim of enhancing the KBUD's knowledge interactions among different actors. The theoretical framework for a generic 'KBU-Land Use Design Model' (KBUD-LUDM) is proposed. Such a model looks at the dynamic KBUD's mixed land uses, utilizing data from Singapore's public authority, the Jurong Town Corporation (JTC), for its 'One North' industrial real estate research park case study. Chapter 3 discusses the KIDC that facilitates and enhances the intra-cluster interaction for post-industrial real estate developments, and the dynamic KBUD-LUDM that offers an alternative flexible approach to traditional land use master planning.

Chapter 4 discusses the design and planning literature of post-industrial clusters. The Chapter even discusses the simulation results and findings of the 'Knowledge-Based Urban Development-Land Use Design Model' (KBUD-LUDM) utilizing Singapore's Biopolis at One North knowledge-based urban development (KBUD). Chapter 4 looks at the basic assumptions of the KBUD-LUDM, which are required to initialize and conduct the scenario analysis. The 'Baseline Scenario' of the One North KBUD adopts the agent initialization procedure (AIP), which is estimated from primary surveys and interviews. The Baseline Scenario is a benchmark to project scenarios of plausible future states of the Biopolis at the One North KBUD. The KBUD-LUDM demonstrates flexibility in conducting incremental planning because land-use demand fluctuates over time. Then validation and visualization procedures looks at future states of the Biopolis at One North KBUD, via the KBUD-LUDM. Chapter 4 also discusses the study approach, the research enquiry, the results and findings. Several directions for extending the KBUD-LUDM via inclusion of multiple design criteria, for comprehensive multi-dimensional land-use design modelling. Lastly, Chapter 5 concludes the entire study.

Chapter 1

Strategic Industrial Real Estate – The Biopolis, Singapore

Singapore, a land-constrained nation, has gradually transformed its economy from a labour-intensive one, heavily reliant on manufacturing industries, into a more service-oriented and, more recently, knowledge-intensive one – all within the past four decades. However, manufacturing is still seen as the traditional engine for growth, which accounts for about 20.9% as far back as 2011, but down from an average of 25.17% from the prior period of 1985 to 2000. The service industry currently makes up about 69% of nominal GDP[i]. From 2000[ii], Industrial land that accommodates the manufacturing and warehousing activities occupy around 12.2% of the total land area on the 710 km² city state island. Similar to other categories of land uses in Singapore, industrial land is predominantly owned by the state, and from 1985 the state owns approximately 76.2%[iii] of all land, supplied to the market via a government land-sales program or other government agencies like the Urban Redevelopment Authority (URA), Housing Development Board (HDB), Port Authority of Singapore (PSA), Land Transport Authority (LTA) and the Jurong Town Corporation (JTC). JTC is Singapore's public sector industrial landlord and is responsible for providing serviced industrial spaces[iv].

Some two decades ago and in recognising the importance of innovation driven growth for its economy, the Singapore government put together the first National Technology Plan (1991-1995), allocating funds for R&D (research and development) infrastructure and human capital development, in a variety of appled scientific fields like microelectronics, semiconductors, electronic systems, manufacturing technology, food and agrotechnology, biotechnology and the medical sciences[v] industries. Such a shift in industrial policy is followed up by a second (1996-2000) and a third (2001-2005) five-year plan of science and technology, giving a boost to the public and private agencies to focus on industrial R&D, to develop new products and to expand markets, taking advantage of fast-growing developing countries like China, India, Indonesia and Thailand. Over time and as observed in Figure 1, there has been a gradual shift in the physical industrial landscape in Singapore, marked by a slow transfer from warehouses and single purpose factories, accommodating manufacturing industries, to the multi-purpose business parks and high-specification facilities, accommodating the knowledge intensive sectors[vi]. Therefore, and such a fast-growing demand for the new investment class of business parks and high-specification facilities, is primarily due to proactive state policies over the last two decades.

Figure 1. The Rising Stock of Hi-Tech Industrial Space In Singapore

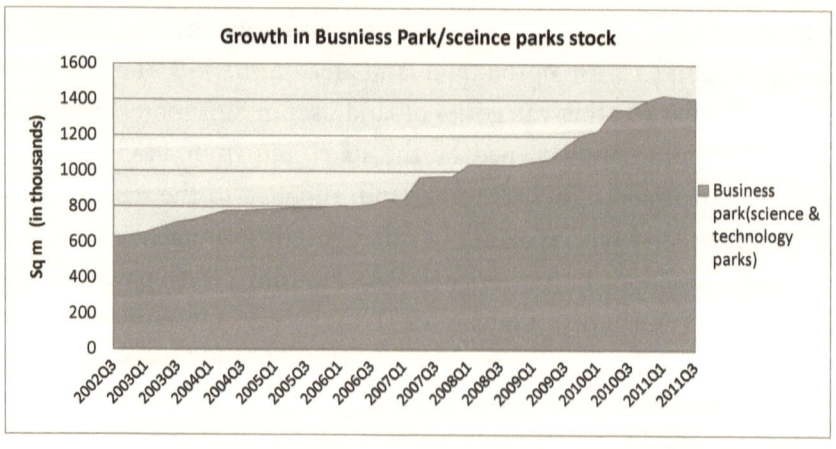

Source: Realis, 2012; Author, 2021

As early as 1991 and owing to favourable forces of globalization and technological innovation, the Singapore government launched the Technopreneurship 21 (T21) program. Consequently, strategic facilities are earmarked to be critical to develop, and so the Biopolis is entrusted to the Jurong Town Corporation (JTC), the nation's industrial master planner, architect and developer (JTC, 2001). Singapore's Biopolis at One North[vii] is a strategic and integrated long term direct real estate development project, designed to serve as an iconic and intellectually stimulating environment, to enable innovative interaction between biomedical researchers and entrepreneurs[viii]. As an integrated spatial locus for the biomedical, information, communications and the technopreneur industries, the One North Biopolis is planned as a highly unique, mixed-use development and to be readily branded with the moniker as the "*Biopolis* of Asia" (Parayil, 2005).

Sustained demand for high-tech industrial accommodation depends heavily on the performance of technologically intensive firms. Whitley (2003) stresses that the combined role of the public science system, industry involvement, the reliance on specialist skills and the ability to change competences radically, are the four different degrees affecting innovative competences and therefore the sustainability of technologically intensive firms. It is well recognized that that changes in all these four degrees are dominantly influenced by state policies, which are directed to foster and support a knowledge-based economy. How these state policies are translated into wealth creation through direct real estate remains unexplored. We lack the understanding on how institutional frameworks vis-à-vis their interaction with macroeconomic conditions, can well determine the investment value of strategic direct real estate"? Chapter 1 looks at the impact of different institutional policies on the value of the One North Biopolis, a strategic and modern industrial real estate. Chapter 1 as looks at the impact of different macroeconomic conditions on the investment viability of the modern One North Biopolis industrial accommodation.

Chapter 1 is therefore organised as follow: the first section outlines the background and motivation. The next (second) section explains how the different intuitional planning measures (economic and urban) by the state, have essentially shaped the direct real estate value of Biopolis in Singapore. The third section discusses the data and investment analysis approach, adopted to evaluate the financial sustainability of the Biopolis. The fourth section adopts the investment model to conduct standard capital budgeting techniques and with a set of assumptions (in Appendix 1.2). Some relaxation some of the prior assumptions to enable the subsequent Monte-Carlo simulations via multivariate copulas. The fifth section discusses Chapter 1's findings and results and concludes with some policy implications.

The Biopolis at North Case Study

The Biopolis at One North is chosen as the appropriate case study because it serves as an ideal example of a large scale modern strategic industrial real estate development in Singapore. Conceptualized in Figure 2, it is essential to look at two integral aspects, which shape the value of such strategic industrial real estate develop, namely

- The role of institutional policies and
- The macroeconomic conditions.

In the case of the Biopolis at One North, the interaction of the two above named integral aspects contribute to a sustainable demand for direct real estate space, in particularly for Phase 1 of the Biopolis since its 2003 completion. From 2012, the Biopolis four phases are completed and that the Biopolis is completing its fifth phase, jointly with private sector participants.

Figure 2. Conceptual Diagram Representing Strategic Industrial Real Estate Value Creation Chain

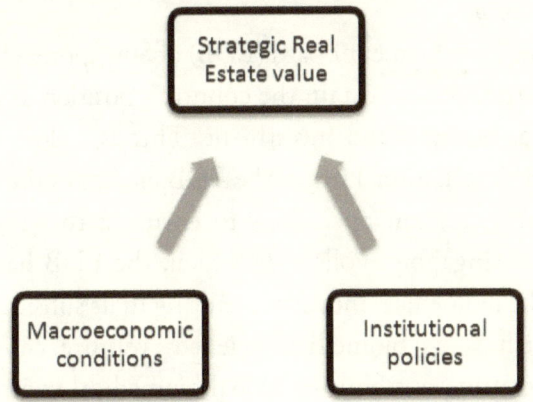

Source: Author, 2021

Chapter 1 first looks at the qualitative analysis regarding the conception and transition of Singapore's industrial policies, where the state's economic and urban planning initiatives are meant to nurture demand for large scale modern strategic industrial real estate development like the One North Biopolis as a new investment asset class. The qualitative analysis helps to understand the different planning facets, meant to sustain demand for the One North Biopolis.

Secondly, Chapter 1 is concerned with the quantitative analysis, where an investment analytical model is adopted to look at the impact of various macroeconomic factors on the financial sustainability of One North Biopolis[ix]. Such an investment analytical model is extended via adopting a dynamic financial analysis (DFA), deploying copula functions to evaluate the risk-return framework for the unique long term strategic One North Biopolis direct real estate investment asset class. The quantitative analysis should help developers and investors to precisely assess the risk-return framework of the emerging class of long term, high-tech and strategic One North Biopolis direct real estate asset class.

The Institutional framework

Economic planning

The Economic Development Board (EDB) of Singapore is tasked to plan and execute strategies to sustain the country's position as a compelling global hub for business and investment. Through close coordination with local and international firms, the EDB facilitates the development of higher value creation operations to ensure a thriving "enterprise ecosystem" in Singapore. Following which, the EDB harvests capital support for the biomedical industry, resulting in its subsidiary, Bio*One Capital, which is its biomedical sciences venture capital arm. Its investment focuses on promising global biomedical companies, where the Bio*One Capital plays a critical role in bridging and supporting the companies' growth strategies, via their Singapore operations. Bio*One Capital offers a strong combination of financial, business, scientific and investment know-how, to enhance the value of companies. Owing to its extensive networks with global pharmaceutical, biotechnological, medical technology firms and venture capitalists, the Bio*One Capital proactively facilitates partnering and collaborative opportunities to enable companies in its portfolio to grow sustainably.

EDB's strategic influence like that on the Biopolis is profound, spans from the incubation of the biomedical sciences industry to establishing spatial infrastructure. Key partners are attracted to generate the foundations of the human capital base, and to offer critical financial support. The strategic influence forms the fundamental basis for the business park direct real estate demand, which in turn supports the net absorption of large scale, strategic, high-tech industrial space like that for the Biopolis at One North. Complementing the EDB's strategic thrust is the Agency for Science, Technological & Research (A*STAR), which focuses on knowledge creation and the exploitation of scientific discoveries to enhance Singapore's scientific competitiveness (A*STAR, 2005).

A*STAR's brainchild, the Biomedical Research Council (BMRC), is established as far back as October 2000 to coordinate Singapore's public sector biomedical R&D activities, via supporting biomedical research and upgrading local human capital in related disciplines. Therefore, A*STAR embarks on enhancing the intellectual capital abilities in key disciplines like the biomedical Sciences, pharmaceuticals, medical technology, biotechnology and healthcare services. A*STAR oversees 14 research institutes and 6 consortia and centres located at One North[x]. Overall, A*STAR and EDB complementarily seek to develop the biomedical sciences cluster into a key pillar of Singapore's economy, developing Singapore's industrial, intellectual and human capital to support the biomedical sciences and related disciplines.

The integrated approach between A*Star and EDB involves various macroeconomic and microeconomic initiatives to support the foregoing disciplines. The approach is conducted by establishing the right physical infrastructure, by providing venture capital support, by strengthening manpower capabilities, and by developing dedicated knowledge based urban development (KBUD). The KBUD serves as a dedicated spatial platform like One north at Biopolis to facilitate the operational needs of incoming participants. In the Biopolis context, the institutional economic and planning strategies continue to have a considerable influence on the demand for dedicated space of the specialized biomedical and related industries. It is not surprising that within 8 quarters, the occupancy rates of the Biopolis at North have surged beyond 90% by 4th quarter 2004, stimulating the impetus for Phase 2 of the Biopolis at One North to commence thereafter. From 2012, Phases 3 and 4 are completed, and that the Biopolis at North is commencing its Phase 5, all of which are jointly developed with private sector participants[xi]. Intuitively, the strategic impact of the institutional policies ultimately forms the fundamental basis for business park demand, to support the net absorption of business park direct real estate space for the Biopolis at One North. Such a strategic impact capitalizes on the Biopolis investment value, crystallizing the effects of broad institutional strategies into tangible large-scale strategic direct real estate investment values.

Urban planning

This section reiterates the influence of industrial urban planning on the One North Biopolis development process by the institutional planning authority, the Jurong Town Cooperation (JTC). The section complements the preceding one with a better understanding of the fundamental causal institutional factors, which shape strategic hi-tech direct real estate structure and behaviour.

> **"Given the fast-changing industrial landscape, JTCs land-use planning approach - its masterplan and land use zoning plans - will have to be highly flexible and quick to adapt to changes in industry, in technology, and in the external environment"**
>
> **- Lee Hsien Loong, Prime Minister of Singapore**

Mirroring PM Lee Hsien Loong's above statement, JTC strategically realigns its planning approach from as far back as September 2001, via promoting industry and enterprise development. JTC duly offers best value industrial facilities. JTC embarked on experimental planning approaches on the Biopolis at One North beyond traditional planning paradigms. JTC has a long history of orchestrating Singapore's industrial landscape, from servicing low-cost land for manufacturing plants to more recently the development of industrial parks to spatially support Singapore's capital-intensive phases of industrialization (1960-1980's).

However, current trends have shifted towards meeting the newer spatial needs of the so called 'knowledge economy'. JTCs' land use planning approaches have moved from the rigid single purpose factories and warehouses to the adaptable, high-tech, experimental and balanced multi-use industrial developments like the Biopolis at One North. On the whole, Singapore's industrial real estate market is in the process of undergoing structural changes, to support the macroeconomic shift from a labour-intensive sector to a high value-added industrial sector.

The Master Plan Phased Development

JTC's development strategy of the Biopolis at One North is to create distinct, yet complementary spatial facilities to enable the provision of an intellectually stimulating and creative physical environment for entrepreneurs, scientists and researchers, to congregate and interact within different phases of the One North Biopolis knowledge based urban development (KUBD) project. For the Biopolis at One North[xii] in Figure 3, it basically revolves around a large 185,000 sq m research complex, accommodating key biomedical research institutes and firms. Incoming firms can take advantage of shared cutting-edge laboratory space, and the firms have access to scientific infrastructure to significantly cut down the R&D costs, and to accelerate the development timeline. Flexible laboratory space sizes ranging from 219 sq m to 1,100 sq m are planned to cater to diverse spatial needs. As part of the mixed used strategy of office and commercial shop spaces, various floor plates are also catered, to complement the knowledge intensive activities.

Figure 3. Illustration Of The Biopolis Master Plan With Predominant Land Uses

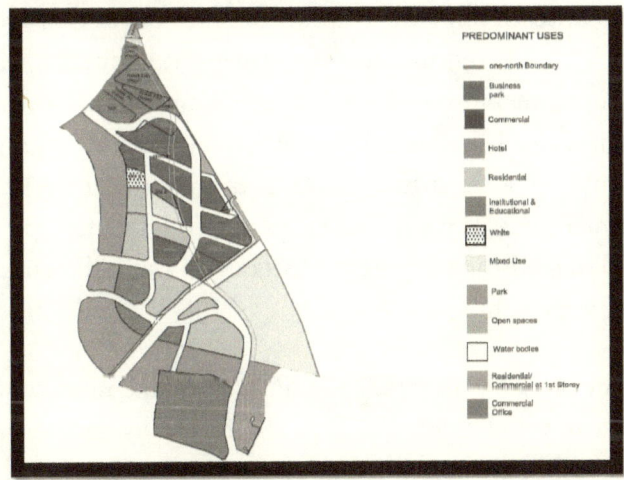

Source: JTC and Author, 2021[xiii]

To be developed in three phases over 15 to 20 years, the Biopolis at One North is planned to be the 200-hectare knowledge based urban development (KBUD), which incorporates unique development strategies. The One North Biopolis (Phase 1) allows for the development of the dynamic core of One North itself, creating a platform for rolling out Phases 2 and 3. The phased development is a financially prudent measure to ensure that such a large-scale strategic direct real estate development is feasible, before embarking on the next phase. The high occupancy rate of 90% of the One North Biopolis in 4th quarter 2004, triggers the subsequent decision to initiate the Phase 2 development at end 2004. The controlled release of business park space in the short and medium term bodes well for the strategic hi-tech investment viability of the business parks, because the limited stock of business park space and the healthy net absorption levels, should pressure due rental values on an upward trajectory. The impact on the overall structure and behaviour of such strategic high-tech industrial real estate is inevitably higher rental values and be capitalized at higher capital values.

The Land Use planning

The land use planning of the Biopolis at One North is largely experimental because JTC incorporates an unprecedented vibrant mix of land uses, to facilitate the Biopolis at One North to be an integrated live-work-play-learn physical environment. Biopolis at One North now consists of a broad land use mix of commercial, industrial, residential and retail uses, enabling a highly interactive and vibrant environment, which boasts of a 24-hour activity cycle. Land use zoning tries to achieve adequate mixing of the different land uses on both the horizontal and vertical dimensions. It is carried out to achieve vibrancy and diversity for the overall landscape. Figure 4 illustrates this multidimensional land use zoning approach.

JTC adopts a flexible approach in Figure 4 to take into consideration unexpected demand fluctuations in the future by making a certain percentage of the land parcels to be "white-site(s)" in their land use plans. Such a flexible approach allows potential private real estate developers to take advantage of orchestrating synergistic developments, where opportunities for an innovative mixed-use development can maximize development value. In short, developers are given greater development autonomy as they may well have a better gauge of potential spatial demand, which can increase realized rents that are further capitalized into higher asset values. Overall, we can see that via the economic and urban planning efforts, the intuitional framework that JTC puts in place, has contributed to attaining a sustainable pace of industrial demand for the Biopolis at One North.

Figure 4. Illustration Of Horizontal And Vertical Land Use Zoning Approach Of The Biopolis

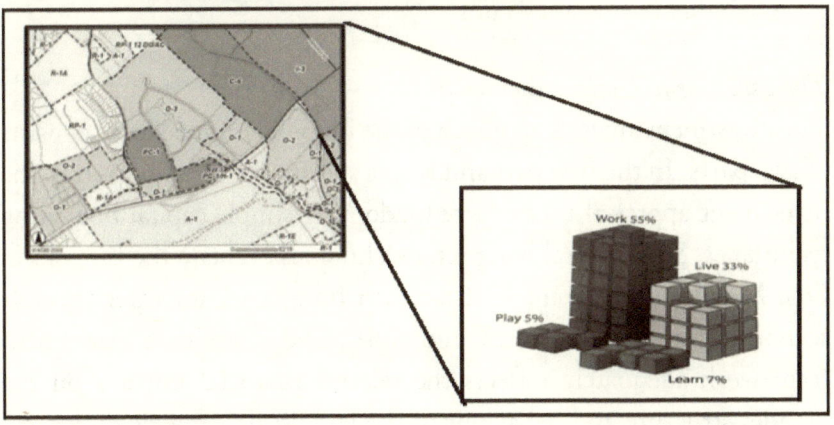

Source: JTC, 2012; Author, 2021

While the preceding subsections reflect how institutional polices, industrial urban planning and the master plan's unique land use design approach can endogenously impact the fundamental investment potential of the Biopolis at One North, the explicit operational feasibility of the Biopolis at One North can be more robustly ascertained, via an investment analysis approach.

The Data and Approach

The Data

We obtain project level data pertaining to the developmental details of the Biopolis at One North from the Jurong Town Cooperation (JTC) (see Appendix-1A). Macroeconomic time series data are accessed via the online DATASTREAM and REALIS (Real Estate Information System). The require data for the period 2001to 2011nclude the following:

- island wide business park and commercial rental yields,
- interest rates,
- inflation and
- industrial vacancy rates.

The Investment Analysis Approach

The investment analysis approach of the Biopolis at One North consists of two parts. In the first part and with a specific set of assumptions, the investment appraisal is conducted, adopting simple capital budgeting techniques, Such capital budgeting techniques evaluate the Biopolis at One North via a systematic risk-return framework for three possible scenarios (in Appendix 1.2 and 1.4). The systematic risk-return framework adequately reflects the relative financial impacts on the broader structure and behaviour of the large-scale strategic direct real estate fundamentals. The systematic risk-return framework is extended from a three-scenario framework to a multiple scenario framework, adopting Monte Carlo techniques. In the second part, a dynamic financial analysis (DFA) model is constructed, which is similar to the one proposed by Kaufmann *et al.* (2001).

The DFA of Figure 5 involves the assignment of multivariate copula distributions among selected and uncertain variables of the DFA model, which are believed to co-vary over time. The modified investment model fitted with the copulas is subjected to the Monte Carlo simulated estimations, for depicting a more realistic scenario. The central idea of both the copulas and the Monte Carlo simulated approaches is meant to quantify whether or not the investment is able to meet its future commitments in probabilistic terms, under different economic conditions. Results from both approaches are compared and inferences are drawn from them. Figure 5 shows the steps involved in the investment analysis approach for Chapter 1. To validate the extent to which the institutional framework and the macroeconomic conditions, tangibly shape the fundamental financial structure and behaviour of the Biopolis at One North. The investment analysis is conducted via adopting standard capital budgeting and risk assessment techniques.

Figure 5. The Flow Diagram of Investment Analysis Approach

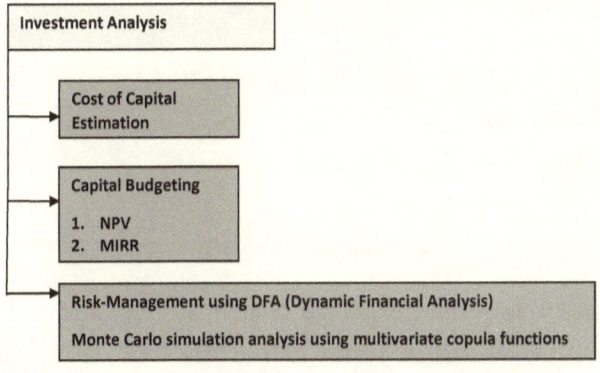

Source: Author, 2021

Capital Budgeting – The Cost of Capital Estimation

The cost of capital or the minimum required rate of return is crucial for capital budgeting decisions. The criteria concerned correlates the perceived project risks and seeks to ensure that stakeholders like the JTC is adequately compensated for undertaking business risks for developing large-scale strategic direct real estate projects like the Biopolis at One North.

The weighted average cost of capital (WACC) is the weighted average cost of equity of a large-scale strategic direct real estate project. The WACC is adopted to discount the project's average cash flow, to obtain its Net Present Value (NPV). Intuitively, the discount augments the investment appraisal regarding the relative profitability of comparable projects. In the case of the large-scale strategic Biopolis at One North project, its equity financing source is assumed to originate from retained earnings, and from the medium-term bond issues for its debt financing. To ascertain the cost of capital (K_p), the Capital Asset Pricing Model (CAPM), which measures the relationship between risk and the project's expected return, is adopted. The cost of capital (K_p) is expressed in the eq (1).

$$K_e = R_f + \beta_p (R_m - R_f) \tag{1}$$

, where,

K_e = Project's cost of equity or expected return
R_f = Risk-free rate
β_p = Project's beta
R_m = Expected market return

The CAPM expresses the expected returns of the large-scale strategic Biopolis at One North in terms of the risk-free rate-of-return (R_f), measured by the 10-year Government securities bond yield rate, in addition to a risk premium, measured by the expected market return over the prevailing risk-free premium ($R_m - R_f$). The risk

R_f	R_m	β_p
3.71%	7.34%	0.77

premium is subject to the market beta (β_p), which measures the market risk. For the large-scale strategic Biopolis at One North, the average common stock prices of 6 major direct real estate firms. listed on the domestic Straits Times Index just before the developmental stage period (of 2001) is utilised as the proxy for the expected market return. As the CAPM model (in Appendix-1.3) indicates the relative components, which derive the project's cost of equity (K_e), the CAPM model would equate to a value of 6.51%. To derive the cost of capital (K_p), eq (2) is adopted.

The Biopolis at One North Capital Asset Pricing Model (CAPM)

$$K_p = K_e \left[\frac{E}{D + E} \right] + K_d \left[\frac{D}{D + E} \right] \quad\quad (2)$$

Where,

K_p = Cost of capital
K_d = After tax cost of debt = Cost of Debt (1-Marginal Tax Rate)
D = Debt value in Financing
E = Equity value in Financing

Combining the CAPM variables and their values with the expected return at 6.51 %, the resultant large-scale strategic Biopolis at One North's cost of capital or the required hurdle rate of return (K_p), is estimated at 6.13 %.

Such a favourable expected return validates the positive impacts of JTC's institutional measures. Since the expected return (K_e) exceeds the required return (K_d), and from a simple capital budgeting standpoint, the Biopolis at One North is deemed to be a viable large-scale strategic direct real estate development project. JTC is expected to be compensated with positive abnormal returns for undertaking the prevailing project and market risks.

The Net Present Value (NPV)
The NPV kind of investment appraisal accounts for the present value of future cash inflows and outflows at the prevailing discount rate. The large-scale strategic Biopolis at One North project should be accepted if NPV is positive. With reference to Appendix-1.4, the positive NPV of the Biopolis at One North project is S$67,365,726 and broadly indicating that the institutional and macroeconomic conditions do positively shape the investment cash flows of the Biopolis at One North via enhancing the absorption rate of its space.

The Modified Internal Rate of Return (MIRR)

The MIRR kind of investment appraisal method discounts the net present value of cash flows to zero and measures the worth of an investment in terms of the expected return. Crucially, the MIRR should ideally be both positive and above the cost of capital. The MIRR is generally indicative of a project's ability to compensate abnormal returns at the prevailing market risk levels. For the large-scale strategic Biopolis at One North project, the after-tax MIRR (ATMIRR) is adopted for the project's investment appraisal. With reference to Appendix-1.4, the ATMIRR of 8.511% surpasses the required rate of return, indicating a favorable opportunity cost of capital for the large-scale strategic Biopolis at One North project. The positive NPV together with the high MIRR override the cost of capital, signaling the favorable investment project viability.

The Multivariate Copula Risk Analysis for The Biopolis at One North

Capital budgeting and risk management and are two key components of the investment decision process. Their interaction enables them to jointly determine owing to their dependent risk exposures, and the synergistic relationships among the crucial economic variables in a dynamic business environment (Jing & Tianyang, 2012). The proper accounting for uncertainty of the input and output variables in an investment analytical model is crucial in risk assessment. The 'What if' scenario analysis is widely used in quantitative risk analysis but such a scenario analysis has several limitations, compared to other risk analysis techniques (Kaufmann *et al.*, 2001).

Such simple scenario analysis assumes equal probability weighting for all the scenarios. Less recognition is accorded to identifying those scenarios, which are more likely to occur than others. A more realistic technique would be to model the problem over multiple scenarios with greater emphasis on incorporating the relative uncertainty of the investment variables. Measures like assigning probability distributions to the uncertain variables, based on their expected behaviour (either historical or forecasted), and accounting for the interdependent behaviour of economic and financial variables, would make the risk analysis more realistic and robust (Biller & Gunes, 2010; Vose, 1996). To mitigate these inherent limitations, a dynamic financial analysis (DFA) model is constructed. In Figure 6, the DFA model takes into consideration the potentially large number of probabilistic scenarios for the uncertain variables.

Defining the Copulas

To account for the inter-dependency issues among uncertain variables, the DFA model is enhanced by introducing copula functions, to consider the correlation among the selected endogenous variables over time. Failure to do so leads to observing wrong joint probabilities of two or more variables in the risk analysis model (Vose, 1996). In Figure 6, the Monte Carlo model simulation estimation acts as the stochastic scenario generator, which essentially assigns each uncertain variable with a unique probability distribution. Some other advantages of the Monte Carlo simulation estimation comprise the following (Vose, 1996):

- Distributions of uncertain variables need not be approximated in any way.
- Correlation and interdependencies among the financial variables can be modelled.
- Greater levels of precision owing to many iterations and that the
- Model is modifiable and adaptable to complex mathematical functions.

As suggested by Vose (1996), the effect of the correlations or interdependencies among the input variables of the Monte Carlo simulation estimation has a great impact on the model estimation. Neglecting such correlations among the variables of the investment (DFA) model leads to wrong joint probabilities. Recent progress in copula functions offers a powerful approach of capturing the correlations or dependencies among the uncertain variables. Copula functions, first introduced by Sklar (1996) in the field of survival analysis and actuarial sciences, has gained momentum in finance and credit market applications by Li (1999), making the copula function an essential tool in risk management and modelling.

Figure 6. Structure Of The DFA Model

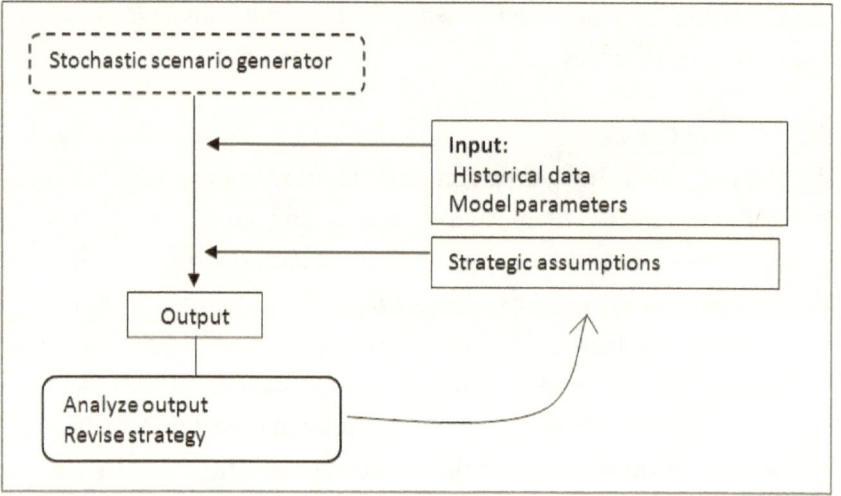

Source: Kaufmann *et al.*, 2001 and Author (2021)

The Sklar (1996) theorem states that any joint cumulative multivariate distribution function is derived in terms of a copula and its continuous marginal distributions. Usually, such inter-relatedness among the variables is captured using a simple correlation coefficient. Unfortunately, this inter-relatedness only works with variables for the normal distributions. When variables tend to be skewed, then copulas better represent the inherent relationship among two or more variables. In simple terms, if the individual distribution functions are known then an unknown joint distribution function is derived using a copula. Such a fitted distribution function captures the correlation and the co-movement among two or more variables through time.

In a statistical sense, copulas link individual univariate marginal distributions of a set of random variables, to form joint multivariate distributions, to capture the interdependency of data points between variables. Therefore, and in simple terms, assigning such copulas is one way of specifying a relationship between random variables. The complete set of variables, deemed to be uncertain for the large-scale strategic Biopolis at One North investment analysis model, include the following:

1) rental yields,
2) interest rates,
3) inflation,
4) LTV (loan-to-value ratio),
5) vacancy and collection lose,
6) sales costs,
7) taxes and
8) operating expenses.

We know from our scenario analysis that all the above 8 variables have a significant impact on the IRR and NPV. The investment analysis of the large-scale strategic Biopolis at One North defines the multivariate copula functions for:

• interest rates,
• inflation,
• rental yields and
• vacancy rates,

based on historical data. Table 1 presents the list of descriptive statistics for those variables, which are adopted to run our model simulation estimation for the large-scale strategic Biopolis at One North investment risk analysis.

Table 1. Descriptive Statistics Of Variables Used For Monte Carlo Simulations

Input Variables	Range	Distribution
LTV	60-90%	Triangular
Inflation	0.5-5%(historical[xiv])	Student3[xv]*
Interest rate	2-5 % (historical)	Student3*
Vacancy	5-15 % (historical)	Lognormal*
OPE	20-35%	Triangular
Taxes	15-25%	Triangular
Sales cost	1.5-4%	Triangular
Rental yields	S$ 2.3-4.4 (Historical)	Lognormal*
* Copulated multiple series adopting the Vose model risk multivariate copula function.		

Source: Author, 2021

The first column of Table 1 represents the list of chosen uncertain variables for the large-scale strategic Biopolis at One North investment risk analysis. The second column provides the "range" of uncertainty for each input variable assigned via either simple assumptions or utilising available historical data. The third column shows each type of unique distribution, assigned to each uncertain variable. Figure 7 depicts the 13-period forecasts of the variables with their assigned copula functions. Such variables are deployed for the large-scale strategic Biopolis at One North investment analytical model (see Appendix 1.5).

Figure 7. Aggregated Yearly Simulated Data Utilising Multivariate Copula Distributions

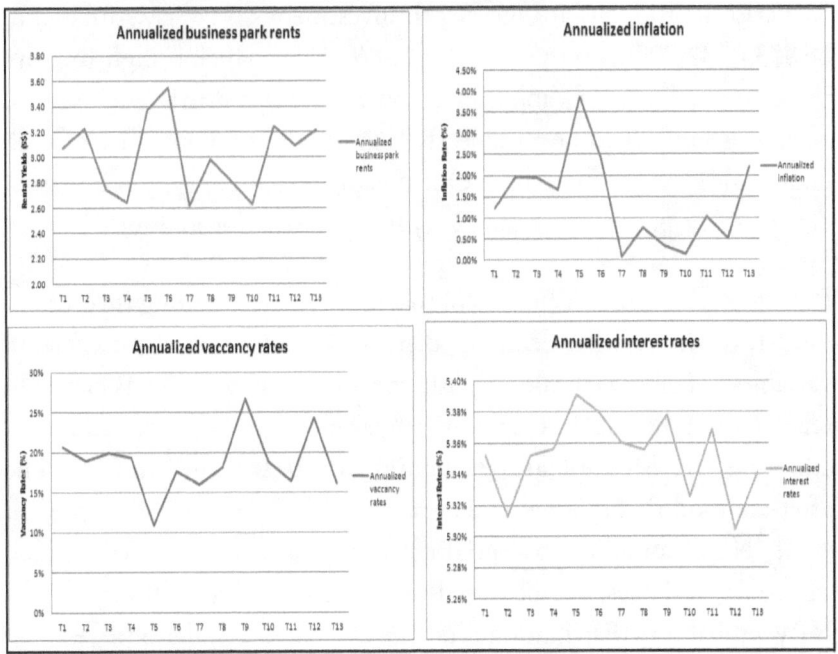

Source: Author, 2021

As the quantity theory of money suggests, a negative correlation is found between inflation and interest rates in Singapore i.e. as the money supply goes up, then tighter monetary policies are imposed by MAS (Monetary Authority of Singapore), to curb rising and high inflation via higher interest rates. Similarly, rental yields and vacancy rates have an inverse relationship in Singapore, a natural long term phenomenon, which occurs as the direct real estate space and asset markets interact over time (DiPasquale & Wheaton, 1996).

Results and Findings

The large-scale strategic Biopolis at One North investment analytical model is estimated for three scenarios, namely the 'Optimistic, Pessimistic and Neutral Scenarios' (Appendix 1.3). The effect of each scenario on the NPV and the IRR of the large-scale strategic Biopolis at One North are examined. It is inferred that even during the Pessimistic Scenario the Biopolis at One North investment's NPV is estimated to be S\$34,432,702 with the ATMIRR of 6.812%, which is slightly above the estimated cost of capital of 6.13%. The Optimistic and Neutral Scenarios both yield favourable IRRs, validating the viability of such large-scale strategic Biopolis at One North and similar type of investing development projects by the JTC (Jurong Town Corporation).

Relaxing the prior 3-scenario approach, the corresponding investment model is fitted with realistic distributions for all the uncertain variables (of Table 1), along with the multivariate copulas between related variables. Such a dynamic investment model is re-estimated, adopting the Monte-Carlo simulation of 10,000 iterations[xvi]. The after-tax modified internal rate of return (ATIRR) and the net present value (NPV) for all the potential risks or variations concerned with all uncertain variables, are observed and recorded. Figure 8 depicts the NPV probability distribution after the estimated simulation.

Figure 8. Results Of Possible Values of NPV After Ten Thousand Iterations

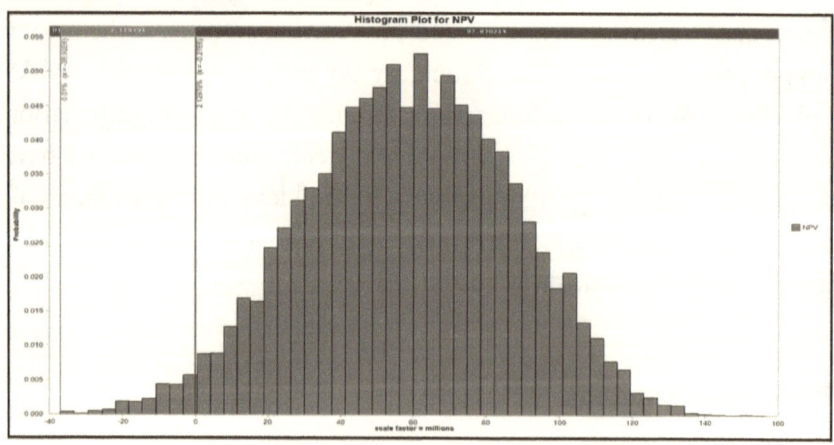

Source: Author (2021)

The minimum NPV achieved is a negative S$40 million[xvii] but the probability of such an event is very small (less than 2.11%). However, the simulated net present values (NPVs) of the large-scale strategic Biopolis at One North, show that there is a high probability (84%) of the NPV being between S$20 and 100 million[xviii]. To gauge the magnitude of the impact of other uncertain variables on the NPV, a graphical spider plot is depicted in Figure 9. The spider plot shows the conditional mean NPV in S$, with respect to the change (in percentile) of each random variable. In other words, Figure 9 shows the impact of macroeconomic fluctuations on the NPV for a large-scale strategic direct real estate development project like the Biopolis at One North.

Figure 9. Spider Plot of NPV Showing Sensitivity With Other Variables

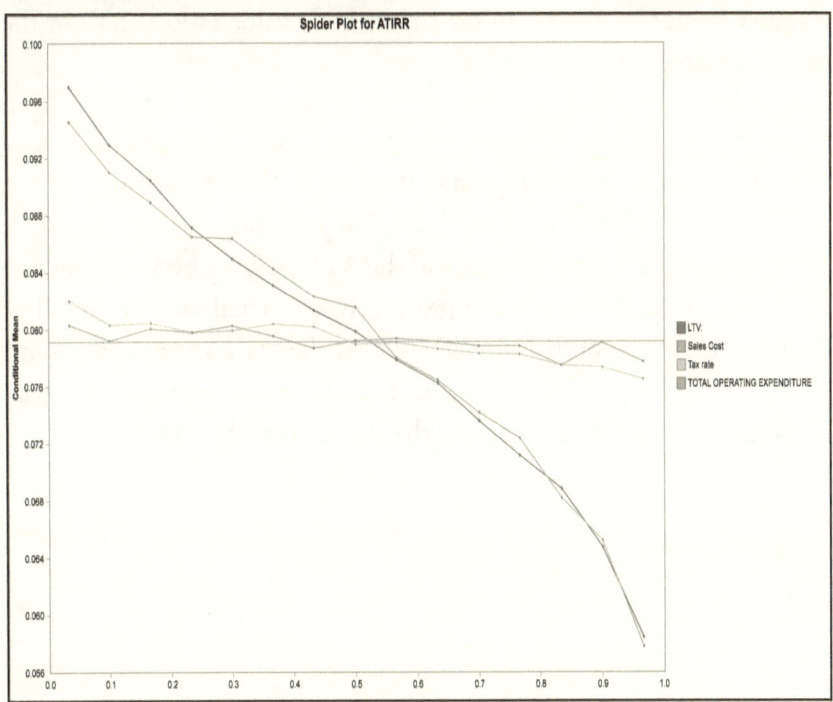

Source: Author, 2021

From the simulated model estimations, the operating cost and the loan-to-value ratio have a significant impact on the net present value (NPV) in Figure 9. For e.g. a rise in operating expenditure from the 10th percentile (0-10%)[xix] to the 90th percentile[xx] (90-100%), while holding everything else constant, would reduce the conditional mean of the NPV by almost S$87 million to S$22 million, an almost 74.71 % fall.

Direct real estate developers may well be prompted to introduce green technology into large-scale strategic industrial real estate development projects like the Biopolis at One North, to save on operating costs over the short to medium term. The magnitude of the impact, caused by the corporate tax rates and sales tax rates on the NPV and the internal rate of return (IRR), does not seem to affect the development project viability by much, relative to say the loan-to- value ratio (LTV) or the operating expenditure (OPE).

From Figure 10, the after-tax internal rate of return (ATIRR) also remains positive, indicating that there is a 23% probability of the ATIRR being below 7% and with a 6.3% probability of it being above 10%; and with a 70% probability of the ATIRR lying between 7% and 10%. The ATIRR exceeds the previously estimated cost of capital of 6.13% with a 91% probability. Therefore, there are strong indications of favourable returns for the case of the large-scale strategic industrial real estate investment project like the Biopolis at One North.

Figure 10. Results Of Possible Values of The ATIRR After 10,000 Iterations

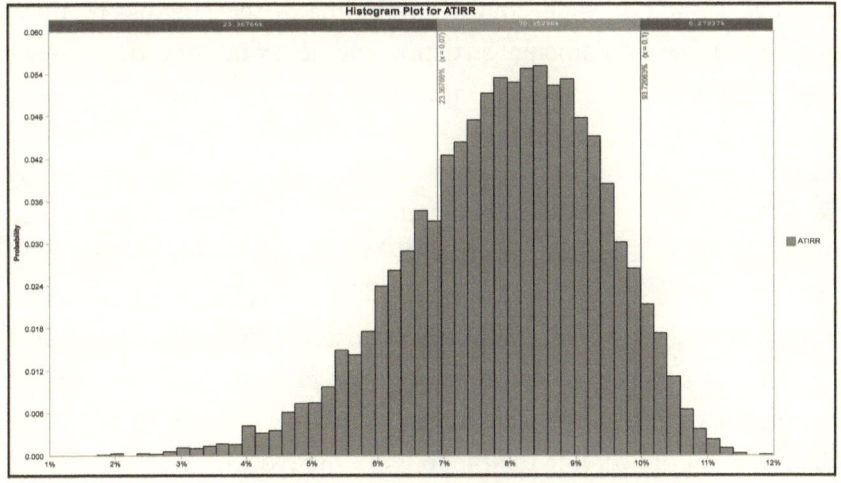

Source: Author (2021)

Concluding Comments

Chapter 1 explores qualitatively and quantitatively the extent to which the fundamental structure and behaviour of the large-scale high-tech strategic industrial real estate development project, can be shaped in terms of the institutional and macroeconomic conditions. A conceptual model is proposed of how such a large-scale strategic high-tech direct real estate development project, is shaped for Singapore's Biopolis at One North. Macroeconomic and institutional strategies by the EDB (Economic Development Board) and A*STAR (Agency for Science, Technology & Research), are found to influence the human, industrial and intellectual capital components of the Biopolis at One North.

The JTC (Jurong Town Corporation) has instrumentalised the physical mould of the Biopolis at One North via JTC's master planning and urban design strategies. Such foregoing government agencies morph the fundamental investment value of the large-scale high-tech strategic Biopolis at One North development project, because the project affects demand for dedicated and specialized biomedical space in the space market. All the corresponding impacts are captured in an investment analytical model, which empirically estimates the tangible financial impacts on the fundamental structure and behaviour of the large-scale high-tech strategic industrial real estate at the project level.

From Figure 10, the investment analysis, adopting capital budgeting techniques, shows a positive net present value (NPV), and a high enough after-tax internal rate of return (ATMIRR), in which the expected returns exceed the required returns. The risk analysis via adopting copula functions affirms the relative impact (in probabilistic terms) of the various uncertain macroeconomic and financial variables, on the profitability of the large-scale high-tech strategic industrial real estate development project like the Biopolis at One North.

Chapter 1 affirms the case of the Biopolis at One North for Singapore, in which favourable and sustainable industrial real estate market outlooks, relevant macroeconomic institutional policies and industrial urban plans, do positively shape the fundamental structure and value of large-scale high-tech strategic industrial real estate. More importantly, the extent to which the foregoing institutional policies can be reasonably expected to yield favourable risk-return investment values for large-scale high-tech strategic industrial real estate development projects, has been rigorously examined to be highly plausible via empirical evidence. Chapter 1 should be of primary interest to private and public listed real estate developers and policy makers, in bettering their understanding of the risk-return framework of such unique, large-scale high-tech strategic industrial real estate development projects like the Biopolis at One North.

Figure 10. Distribution Of ATIRR From Monte-Carlo Simulations (Involving 10,000 Iterations)

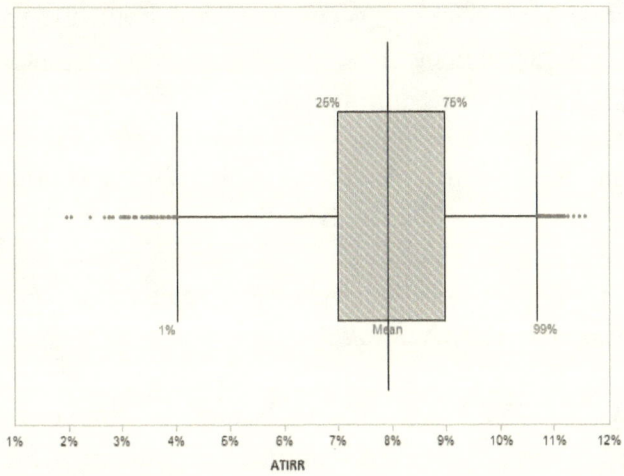

Source: Author, 2021

(The author wishes to acknowledge his appreciation to Dr Rengarajan Satyanarain, a former NUS research scholar, and presently a management information system consultant; for his dynamic perseverance and contribution in sourcing the related literature, the required primary and secondary data and treatment, and for the initial analysis).

References

A*STAR. (2005). Annual R & D survey 2003-2009. Singapore: Agency for Science, Technology and Research., from http://www.a-star.edu.sg/astar/about/action/about_astar_pub_annualrnd.doc

Biller, B., & Gunes, C. (2010, 5-8 Dec. 2010). *Introduction to simulation input modeling.* Paper presented at the Simulation Conference (WSC), Proceedings of the 2010 Winter.

DiPasquale, D., & Wheaton, W. C. (1996). Urban economics and real estate markets. *New Jersey.*

Jing, A., & Tianyang, W. (2012). *Enterprise Risk Management and Capital Budgeting under Dependent Risks: An Integrated Framework. Working paper.* Retrieved from http://www.soa. org/library/monographs/other-monographs/2012/april/mono-2012-as12-1-wang-summary.aspx

Kaufmann, R., Gadmer, A., & Klett, R. (2001). Introduction to dynamic financial analysis. *Astin Bulletin, 31*(1), 213-250.

Li, D. X. (1999). On default correlation: a copula function approach. *Available at SSRN 187289.*

Parayil, G. (2005). From" Silicon Island" to" Biopolis of Asia": Innovation Policy and Shifting Competitive Strategy in Singapore. *California Management Review, 47*(2), 50-73.

Sklar, A. (1996). Random variables, distribution functions, and copulas: A personal look backward and forward. *Lecture Notes-Monograph Series*, 1-14.

Vose, D. (1996). *Quantitative risk analysis: a guide to Monte Carlo simulation modelling*: Wiley Chichester.

Whitley, R. (2003). Competition and pluralism in the public sciences: the impact of institutional frameworks on the organisation of academic science. *Research Policy, 32*(6), 1015-1029.

Wong, K. W., & Bunnell, T. (2006). New economy'discourse and spaces in Singapore: a case study of one-north. *Environment and Planning A, 38*(1), 69.

Zhu, J. (2002). Industrial globalisation and its impact on Singapore's industrial landscape. *Habitat International, 26*(2), 177-190.

Appendix-1.1: Descriptive statistics – Biopolis Phase 1

Parcel	Life Exchange (Biopolis)
Site Area (sq m)	39,908
Plot Ratio	4.65
GFA (sq m)	
Business Park	180,173
Commercial	5,000
Total	185,173
GFA (sq ft) '000	1,993
Efficiency Ratio	70.00%
NFA (sq m)	
Business Park	126,121
Commercial	3,500
Total	129,621
NFA (sq ft) '000	
	1,358
Business Park	38
Commercial	
Total	1,395
Land Value (S$ psf PPR)	
Business Park	$73
Commercial	$73
Land Value (Estimated S$)	
Business Park	
Commercial	141,573,720
Total	3,928,827
	145,502,548

Source: JTC, 2005; Author, 2021.

Appendix-1.2: Biopolis Cash Flow Statement Assumptions

- Construction start stage for Biopolis 2001(4Q) and construction takes 20 months

Land Value
- Industrial land value based on median land price of 60 year leasehold in Year 2000

WACC
- Debt Finance through Medium Term Bond Issue, due 2005-2012 at 5% p.a. interest
- Equity Finance through Retained Earnings

Revenue
- Average Annual Rental projected to grow at 3% p.a.
- Forecasted quarterly growth based on moving average

Expenditure
- Total Expenditure constitutes 30% of EGI

Tax
- Corporate tax constant throughout holding period
- Property tax subsumed under total expense, constituting a portion of Total Expense = 30% EGI

Reversion
Reversion upon Bond redemption in end of year 2012 (As stated in JTC Financial Statements 2004)

Scenario Analysis

Scenario	Neutral	Optimistic	Pessimistic
Rental Rate	Determined by average annual rental forecast at 3% inflation	Inflation adjustment at 3% on Total Revenue	Inflation adjustment at 1% on Total Revenue
VCL	10% first 5 years, 5% thereafter	5% throughout holding period	10% throughout holding period
Operating Expense	30% of EGI initially, 1% annual inflation thereafter	30% of EGI initially, 0.5% annual inflation thereafter	30% of EGI initially, 1.5% annual inflation thereafter
LTV	70.00%	60.00%	80.00%

Appendix-1.3: Biopolis Capital Asset Pricing Model

Normal Probability Plot of Residuals

JTC (Ascendas) Return = 0.770 Market Return + 0.025
R2 = 0.7878

JTC (Ascendas) Return (%) vs Sample Property Market Return (Percentile)

◆ JTC (Ascendas) Return — Linear (JTC (Ascendas) Return)

Using CAPM to find Beta

Comparison of Stock / Bond Prices

Name	ASCENDAS US$	%	CCT US$	%	CDL US$	%	KEPPELAND US$	%	MCL LAND US$	%	SINGAPORE LAND US$	%	Sum of TR %	Average %
1Q2004	0.688	0.00%			2.965	0.00%	1.084	0.00%	0.855	0.00%	2.379	0.00%	0.00%	0.00%
2Q2004	0.787	14.39%			2.71	-8.60%	1.084	0.00%	0.875	2.34%	2.31	-2.90%	5.23%	1.05%
3Q2004	0.875	11.18%			3.405	25.65%	1.027	-5.26%	0.816	-6.74%	2.536	9.78%	34.61%	5.77%
4Q2004	0.962	9.94%	1.08	0.00%	3.676	7.96%	1.058	3.02%	0.861	5.51%	2.69	6.07%	48.25%	8.04%
1Q2005	1.127	17.15%	1.25	15.74%	4.153	12.98%	1.503	42.06%	1.063	23.46%	3.359	24.87%	127.72%	21.29%
2Q2005	1.229	9.05%	1.34	7.20%	4.126	-0.65%	1.444	-3.93%	1.232	15.90%	3.337	-0.65%	28.67%	4.78%
3Q2005	1.369	11.39%	1.46	8.96%	5.262	27.53%	1.75	21.19%	0.893	-27.52%	3.489	4.55%	39.21%	6.53%
4Q2005	1.198	-12.49%	1.49	2.05%	4.986	-5.25%	2.195	25.43%	0.832	-6.83%	3.098	-11.21%	-9.67%	-1.61%
1Q2006	1.279	6.76%	1.5	0.67%	5.317	6.64%	2.422	10.34%	1.07	28.61%	3.657	18.04%	77.06%	12.84%

Average Mkt Return 7.34%

Source: Datastream / UOB Kay Hian

To find Risk Free Rate

Name	S'PORE GOVT LONG TERM BOND YIELD S$	%
1995	100.76	2.80%
1996	108.904	3.30%
1997	109.707	4.60%
1998	112.13	4.10%
1999	119.692	4.20%
2000	124.218	3.80%
2001	132.662	3.70%
2002	136.186	2.10%
2003	149.814	3.20%
2004	150.848	2.30%
2005	152.654	3.00%

Source: EIU Country Data

Total returns 37.10%
Average returns 3.71%

WACC, Finding Hurdle Rate

$Ko = Ke \times [(E/(D+E)] + Kd \times [(D/(D+E)]$

where

Ko = Weight average cost of capital
Ke = Cost of Equity = $Rf + \beta(Rm - Rf)$ = 3.71% + 0.77(7.34% - 3.71%) = 6.51%
Kd = After Tax Cost of Debt = $Ki(1 - t)$ = 5.00% (1 - 20%) = 4%
D = Amount of debt = 70%
E = Amount of equity = 30%

Ko = 6.51% x 0.3 + 4% x 0.7 = 4.753%

Ke > Ko > Kd
6.51% > 6.13% > 4%

Source: Author's estimates, 2012 and 2021

Appendix-1.4: Biopolis Neutral Scenario Cash Flow Estimates

Life Exchange (Biopolis) Phase 1
REVENUE & EXPENDITURE

General Inputs:	
Building Value:	354,497,452
Land Value:	145,502,548
Total Value:	500,000,000
Construction (months):	20

Financial Inputs:	
LTV:	70.00%
Equity:	150,000,000
Beginning Loan Amt:	350,000,000
Ending Loan Amt:	350,000,000
Interest Rate:	5.00%
Term:	8
Annual PMT	8,750,000

Capitalization:	
Terminal Cap Rate	6.00%
Selling Price	557,189,453
Sales Cost	2.00%
Total NFA (sq ft)	1,395,230
Inflation:	1.00%
Vacancy & Collection Losses:	2004-2007 10.00%
	2008 onwards 5%

Reversion Calculation	
Terminal Cap Rate	6.00%
Selling Price	557,189,453
Less: Sales Cost (2%)	11,143,789
Net Sales Proceeds	546,045,664
Less: Bond Payout	₱350,000,000
Equity Reversion	196,045,664

	2001	2002	2003	2004	2005	2006	2007	2008	2009	2010	2011	2012	2013
REVENUE:													
Base Rental Revenue													
Business Park			39,667,793	38,527,446	39,693,269	40,873,767	42,099,980	43,362,979	44,663,869	46,003,785	47,383,898	48,805,415	
Commercial			1,321,216	1,329,128	1,369,001	1,410,072	1,452,374	1,495,945	1,540,823	1,587,048	1,634,659	1,683,699	
TOTAL REVENUES			40,989,009	39,856,573	41,062,270	42,283,839	43,552,354	44,858,924	46,204,692	47,590,833	49,018,558	50,489,115	
Vacang & Collection Losses			4,098,901	3,985,657	4,105,227	4,228,384	2,177,618	2,242,946	2,310,235	2,379,542	2,450,928	2,524,456	
EFFECTIVE GROSS INCOME			36,890,108	35,870,916	36,947,043	38,055,455	41,374,736	42,615,978	43,894,457	45,211,291	46,567,630	47,964,659	
OPERATING EXPENSES													
TOTAL OPERATING EXPENSES 30%			11,067,032	10,888,888	11,194,954	11,530,803	12,536,545	12,912,641	13,300,021	13,699,021	14,109,982	14,533,292	
NOI			25,823,076	25,092,028	25,752,089	26,524,652	28,838,191	29,763,337	30,594,437	31,512,270	32,457,638	33,431,367	
Less: Debt Service (interest expense on bond issues)			8,750,000	8,750,000	8,750,000	8,750,000	8,750,000	8,750,000	8,750,000	8,750,000	8,750,000	0	
BTCF	-150,000,000		25,823,076	16,342,028	17,002,089	17,774,652	20,088,191	21,013,337	21,844,437	22,762,270	23,707,638		
Less: Tax 20%			5,164,615	3,250,406	3,400,418	3,554,930	4,017,638	4,190,667	4,368,887	4,552,454	4,741,528	25,011,367	
Equity / Reversion	-150,000,000										196,045,664		
ATCF	-150,000,000		20,658,461	13,091,623	13,601,671	14,219,722	16,070,553	16,762,669	17,475,549	18,209,816	215,011,774		

Year	2001	2002	2003	2004	2005	2006	2007	2008	2009	2010	2011	2012	2013
BTCF	-150,000,000												
ATCF	-150,000,000												

BTIRR	3.346%
ATIRR	8.511%
NPV	67,365,726

Source: Author's calculations, 2013 an 2021

Appendix-1.5: Simulated Biopolis Cash Flow Estimates Using Multivariate Copula Functions

Source: Author's Estimates, 2013 and 2021

Chapter 2

Strategic industrial real estate market Dynamics - A VAR Approach, The Singapore Experience

From large scale factories and warehouses, which serve as manufacturing and distribution centres to more recently hi-technology industrial research production centres, churning new designs and products, industrial accommodation has become an essential backbone of any thriving economy. However, it remains one of the least studied topics in the direct real estate literature (Rabianski & Black, 1997), among other sub sectors of the real estate market (housing and office sectors). There are several reasons for this dearth in the literature, ranging from the sheer difficulty of predicting demand to high direct real estate product diversity and locational differences, making the sub sector more diverse than other direct real estate sub sectors, in terms of their functional and demand characteristics.

In many countries, industrial real estate has traditionally been owner occupied suggesting that the industrial space is built by or for its occupants directly, making it a part of the firm's investment decision (Wheaton

& Torto, 1990). Owing to this reason, the speculative portion of this sub-sector remains small compared to the retail or housing markets. Recent trends in the industrialized countries suggest that this structure is changing as firms prefer more rental type facilities, owing to the heavy fixed costs involved in providing 'Hi-spec' facilities (Chow *et al.*, 2002). Although one can draw some parallels to the housing, office and retail real estate sub sectors, the long run relationship between demand created by employment and demographics in those sub-sectors respectively are rather intuitive. To understand the behaviour of the industrial real estate sub-sector, it is necessary to study the sub-sector in a macroeconomic context as industrial real estate price movements are more correlated with national and regional economic performance (Wheaton, 2003).

Singapore, a land constrained nation, has transformed its economy from a labour intensive one, heavily reliant on manufacturing industries, towards a more service oriented and more recently a knowledge intensive economy - all within the past four decades. Manufacturing has been the traditional engine for growth, which as far back as 2001 accounted for about 20.9% of the overall GDP. The manufacturing sector is down from an average of 25.17% from 1985 to 2000[xxi]. However, the service industry currently makes up about 69% share of nominal GDP[xxii]. Industrial land comprises 12.2% as of year 2000[xxiii] on the 710 km^2 city state island.

Much like other categories of land uses in Singapore, industrial land is predominantly owned by the state, and as of 1985 the state owned approximately 76.2%[xxiv] of all land, supplied to the market via the government land sales program or other government agencies like the Urban redevelopment authority (URA), the Housing development board (HDB), Port of Singapore Authority (now known as the Maritime and Port Authority), Land transport authority (LTA) and the Jurong town corporation (JTC), which is the public sector industrial landlord in Singapore and responsible for providing serviced industrial spaces[xxv].

In land constrained Singapore, most of the industrial supply is master planned by the JTC (Jurong Town Corporation), Singapore's public sector industrial landlord. The government plays an important role in maintaining rents and capital values at affordable levels, to keep industrial tenants [manufacturers, services, R&D (research and development)] onshore and leading to rising economic activity. Another important feature of the strategic industrial real estate market is its physical and functional obsolescence. Since Singapore has grown from a labour-intensive industrial society into a 'Hi-tech' (i.e. high technology) capital and more recently into knowledge intensive industrial activities over less than four decades, the rate at which purpose built factories and specific manufacturing plants becoming obsolete would be higher here than recorded in other countries[xxvi]. Manufacturing is still seen as a traditional engine for growth which accounts for about 20.9% from 2011 onwards, down from an average of 25.17% from 1985 to 2000[xxvii].

More recently, the gradual shift in the industrial landscape in Singapore is marked by a slow transfer from warehouses, single purpose factories accommodating the manufacturing, the Information Communication Technologies (ICT), food and other material industries, to the multi-purpose science and business parks, otherwise called 'Hi-spec' facilities. The latter in turn would accommodate the knowledge intensive industries like research and development (R&D), Information communications and software consultancies along with design, media and art industries. Recognizing the importance of innovation driven growth, the Singapore government introduced the first national technology plan as far back as 1991, allocating S$2 billion for R&D infrastructure and human capital development for such fields, like microelectronics and semiconductors, electronic systems, manufacturing technology, food and agro technology, biotechnology and medical sciences. A second (1996-2000) and a third (2001-2005) five-year plan of science and technology gave a boost for industries to focus on industrial R&D, to develop new products and to expand markets, taking due advantage of growing developing neighbours like China, India, Indonesia and Thailand. The R&D expenditure as far back as 2005 in Singapore stood at 2.4%, which still low compared to South Korea (2.9%), Japan (3.1%) and the United States (2.7%). The required manpower is also steadily rising with the number of full time equivalent researchers in Singapore rising by over 11% as far back as 2005, which amounts to more than 90 researchers per 10,000 workers, relative to less than 30 in 1990[xxviii].

As the economy gears for such a shift, demand for this new type of strategic direct real estate should grow in importance. Figure 1 depicts the rise of business park space, relative to other types (factories & warehouses), which caters to the knowledge intensive industries over the last decade. From Figure 1, we see the slow albeit steady emergence of business park space as the new industrial space in Singapore.

Figure 1. Chart Illustrating The Stock Growth Of Business Park Space In Singapore (2002Q3-2011Q3)

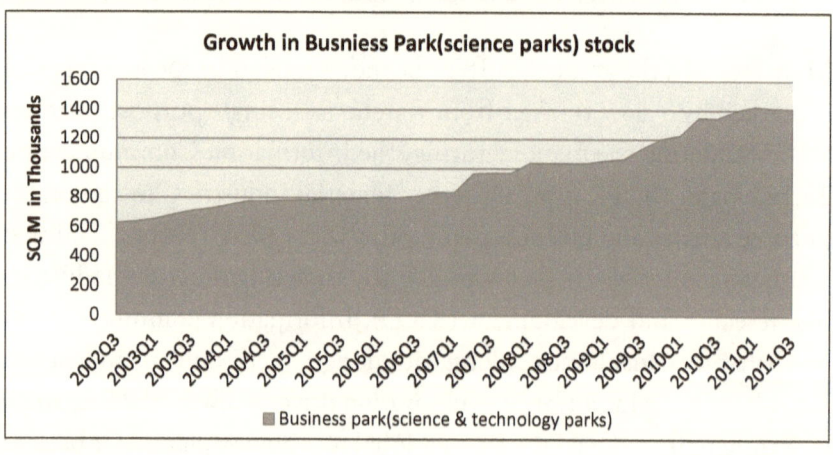

Source: REALIS,2012; Author 2021

To take this new entrant of industrial space in stride, the characteristics of the business parks (or science parks) are incorporated into the overall analysis of the strategic industrial real estate market in Singapore. The behavioural structure of all industrial real estate accommodation is not deemed to exist in a vacuum. Instead, the structure is uniquely shaped through the dynamic interactions of strategic industrial real estate demand-supply conditions, macroeconomic conditions and institutional polices. Together, these elements distinctively influence the demand-supply balance, capital values and rental yields of industrial real estate.

Owing to the unique strategic industrial real estate market in Singapore, there is a lack of understanding on a holistic investment model, which can track changes in the asset and space markets of the strategic industrial real estate market. Since the strategic industrial real estate market is more in tune with the economy and less with the other real estate sub sectors (markets), a pertinent question could be 'Are there unique incubating environments for direct real estate value to be established (i.e. space, asset, investment or development market value) for the strategic industrial real estate market?' If so, how are they shape in the case of Singapore? This can help us to explain a unique direct real estate value determination framework, which can recommend direct real estate value enhancement solutions to stakeholders for wealth expansion activities. It is therefore useful to have an investment model of the supply and demand characteristics for the public and private strategic industrial real estate markets in Singapore.

Chapter 2 discusses a rigorous econometric model estimation, adopting a vector auto regressive (VAR) approach to understand the relationship between the overall industrial net space absorption, vacancy rate, capitalization rates and property price indices, to other macroeconomic variables. The required data set is historical and readily available for research purposes with respect to relevant factors, affecting the behavioural structure of strategic industrial real estate from 2000:Q4 to 2010:Q4. The data set is obtained via authoritative local government agencies like the URA (urban redevelopment authority) and the JTC (Jurong town corporation), international data sources. Secondary private online data agencies include DATASTREAM and Singapore's Real Estate Information System (REALIS), which offer a clear understanding of the dynamic behaviour, which is exhibited by the strategic industrial real estate market in Singapore. Hence, the paper is organized into several sections: the introduction (in the first section) provides the objectives of the study. The next (second) section is concerned with the theoretical framework of direct real estate dynamics, to be followed by the third section's related literature on empirical studies of the strategic industrial real estate market. third section. The third section also discusses the selection of appropriate variables under the VAR model specification. The fourth section discusses the data followed by the estimation results, describing how the island wide strategic industrial real estate market behaves, with respect to differences in macroeconomic demand and supply conditions. The fifth section seeks to understand the interrelationships between strategic industrial real estate and macroeconomic variables, via impulse response and variance decomposition analyses, adopting the VAR model. The sixth section concludes Chapter 2.

The Theoretical Framework

This section offers a comprehensive review of the related institutional and macroeconomic frameworks that enable a conceptualization of the factors, influencing the behavioural structure of te strategic industrial real estate market. The concept of the 'Four-Quadrant Model' by DiPasquale and Wheaton (1996) is introduced.

The stock-flow model of DiPasquale and Wheaton (1996) offers a simultaneous intuitive analysis of the (dis)equilibrium dynamics between direct real estate space, the asset and development markets of an economy (see Figure 2). Spatial demand is derived from the usage of space by firms for production purposes, forming the basis for the direct real estate space market in the northeast quadrant. Determinants of spatial demand by firms hinge on their output levels and the relative cost of space. Central to occupancy cost is rent (R), the annual outlay necessary to obtain the use of real estate, reflecting the space markets fundamentals in the northeast quadrant, which in turn determines how much cash flow a direct real estate asset can generate, and forming its underlying physical asset value that is linked to the wider direct real estate market. Such a market is derived from the ownership of direct real estate and is depicted under the northwest quadrant. Ceteris paribus, when firms expand production and with short-term inelastic supply, real rents (*R*) would rise. The converse holds true.

Figure 2. The Stock-Flow Model of The Direct Real EstateMarket

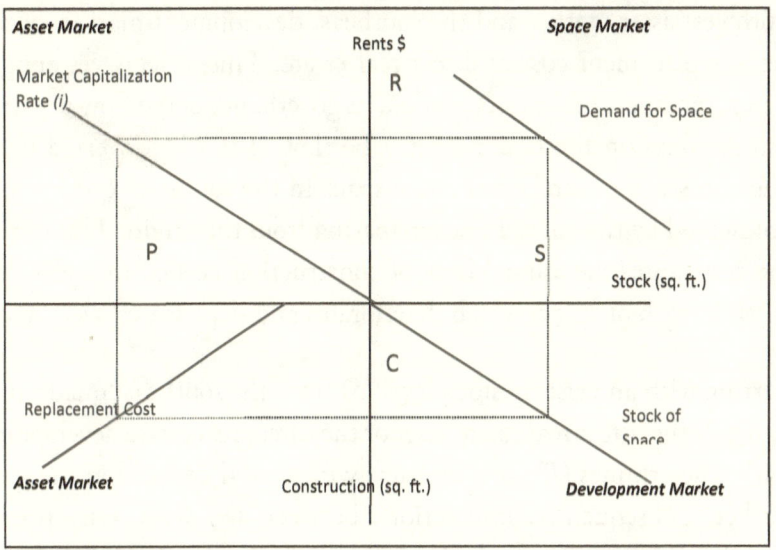

Source: Author, 2021

Asset pricing is also influenced by the market capitalization rate of direct real estate, which is reflected as *(i)* in Figure 2, measuring the direct positive ratio between asset rent-to-price. Figure 2 encapsulates the opportunity cost of capital, future expectations and the risk perceptions of investors. Figure 2 also measures the current yield that investors demand in order to hold direct real estate assets and is represented by eq (2.1).

$$P = \frac{R}{i} \qquad (2.1)$$

Where P = Real estate asset price

R = Rent level
i = Market capitalization rate

The curved line in the southwest quadrant of Figure 2 depicts the replacement cost of direct real estate assets. The curve does not originate from the asset price origin, representing the minimum rate or return, which developers seek for a feasible development to be embarked upon. New construction (C) that is the point of intersection between the southwest asset market and the southeast development market, occurs at the replacement cost of direct real estate. This reflects yet another important aspect of the asset market, its governance of the flow of capital into the direct real estate market. The flow of (C) is converted into a long-run stock of direct real estate space in the southeast quadrant, as represented by the curved line emanating from the origin. This curved line constitutes the annual level of construction needed to replace the existing stock of space, which deteriorates and depreciates over time.

Starting with an existing stock level (S) from the southeast quadrant of Figure 2, the direct real estate asset or the direct real estate development market determines (R), as it interacts with spatial demand in the space market. Subsequently, interactions between (R) with asset pricing capitalization rates (i) determines the asset price (P). Such interaction develops a comparison between replacement cost and (P) in the southwest quadrant, which influences the direct real estate development decision to add new construction (C) to (S) in eqs (2.2) and (2.3) of Figure 2's southeast quadrant.

$$\Delta S = C - \delta S \qquad (2.2)$$

And supply of real estate space is captured as:

$$S = C / \delta \qquad (2.3)$$

Where, S = Stock of real estate

C = New construction
δ = Depreciation

Overall, this stock-flow model explains that the direct real estate markets are in equilibrium when the starting and ending stock levels equate. But with short term adjustments in rent, price and construction, disequilibrium occurs in which long term stock adjustments follows. The stock-flow model serves as the framework of the fundamental dynamics and interactions of the space, the asset and the direct real estate development market of Chapter 2. The stock-flow model of both the space and the direct real estate asset market is a long-run model, given that construction exists.

The stock-flow model's limitations is that it does not trace the intermediate steps as the direct real estate market moves to its new equilibrium, because the task of depicting the intermediate market adjustments requires a dynamic system of equations, which would complicate the analysis. To overcome this limitation with an enhanced understanding of the space and capital markets, the appropriate structural behaviour affecting the pattern and movements of rents and prices can be examined by way of a vector auto regressive (VAR) model. We adopt the VAR model to understand the behaviour of the strategic industrial real estate market for Singapore.

The Related Literature

DiPasquale and Wheaton's (1996) stock-flow model offers a theoretical framework to explain the fundamental equilibrium, the adjusting dynamics and the interactions of the direct real estate space, the direct real estate asset and development market, via short term adjustments in rent, price and construction. Quantitative studies utilizing a set of information regarding the forces that affect demand and supply of space, have proved to be meaningful in empirically estimating the cyclical movements of the strategic industrial real estate market. Such studies aim at identifying key relationships in the direct real estate market that are essentially useful for developers, investors and market regulators (Kling & McCue, 2002; Sing, 2003; Thompson & Tsolacos, 2000; Wheaton & Torto, 1990).

XXXX

There seems to be a predictable cyclical pattern emerging from the literature about the relationship between the macroeconomic conditions and direct real estate market aggregates (Thompson & Tsolacos, 1999). Key variables depicting the behaviour identified widely in the literature are rents and prices (capital values) while industrial rents in turn have been reported to be affected by variables such as gross domestic product, manufacturing output, industrial production, monetary variables (Atteberry & Rutherford, 1993; RICS, 1994; Thompson & Tsolacos, 1999). Thus, theory, intuition and previous empirical findings about different variables affecting the industrial real estate asset and space markets are used to guide our empirical model specification.

Space Market Demand Drivers
With reference to the preceding stock-flow model, the identification and modelling of industrial real estate demand drivers in the space market should firstly be established. These allow the determination of rentals, capitalization rates and capital values in the industrial real estate asset market. The first equation addressing the space market is the amount of new industrial space supplied in the market, as noted by DiPasquale & Wheaton (1999), and is a function of higher levels of profitability. The level of profitability of industrial real estate properties is given by construction costs and Rents (or expected) and also by the business climate at that time period, where the first two exhibit negative and positive effects on the supply and the third a positive outlook respectively (Thompson & Tsolacos, 2000).

Industrial wholesale employment was empirically tested by DiPasquale and Wheaton (1996) as proxies to model industrial net absorption, and was found to be statistically significant. Wheaton and Torto's (1990)'s investment model for the demand and supply of real estate states the precedent proxy has limited significance in determining industrial space demand. Consequently, to mitigate the problem, manufacturing output is used as a proxy. The representation of the manufacturing sector has been found to be statistically significant and less problematic. DiPasquale and Wheaton (1996) have also analysed the relationship between overall industrial productions against the net space absorption in the Philadelphia metropolitan areas. They have found this to be significant, being reinforced by Wheaton and Torto (1990)'s empirical model.

DiPasquale and Wheaton (1996) had empirically tested through a vector error correction model that the change in real GDP is a strong determinant of industrial real estate demand. In Singapore, demand for industrial space is mainly arises from manufacturing (factory and purpose built models), warehousing and more recently knowledge intensive industrial accommodation for industries such as the biomedical, IT services, design, media and arts. Instead of using manufacturing GDP alone as a determinant, we combine this with the share of total (public and private) R&D spending each year since they proxy as an important determinant for generating demand for science and business parks[xxix]. Another demand driver, the *Composite Leading Indicator* (CLI) reflects business confidence and prospects as well as the rational expectations of decision makers.

Kling and McCue (1991) investigated the relationship between industrial property construction and the economy through vector auto regression models, and implicitly highlighted that supply lagged demand. Changes in the *existing stock* could have resulted from a combination of changes in the completion of pipeline stock, vacancy and net absorption.

Asset market demand drivers
Past UK rental yields in the industrial market have been reported to be strongly influencing present values, making them important for the determination of current rents. Rents often travel inverse to occupancy levels in the space market, where a high *vacancy level* indicating less demand would drive rents down in subsequent quarters. A well exhibited phenomenon would be the rent adjustment model using search theory by Wheaton and Torto (1994). More often, the effect of demand pressures in the market translating into changes in rents depends on the degree

of availability of industrial space for occupation. Overall, a negative relationship between floor space availability and rents is evident from historical data in Singapore.

Capital value that encapsulates the opportunity cost of capital, future expectations, risk perceptions and preferences of investors is empirically tested by DiPasquale and Wheaton (1996). They have explained that capital value capture both existing rents *and* expectations of future rental growth. As a result, these factors serve as proxies to forecast capital value through incorporation into the cap rate determinants. The asset market is determined by existing capital values in Singapore with the introduction of the strata industrial title and industrial properties, especially the business parks, are becoming increasingly attractive as investment vehicles.

We use cap rates[xxx] to take into account changes in *capital values* and their associated *rental yields*. This is because in theory the market cap rates tells us two things, firstly that the more demand for the asset as an investment, then the lower would be the cap rate. Secondly, the higher the rental yields compared to the purchase price, then the higher is the cap rate that in the medium to long term can bring in more supply as the replacement cost goes down.

Space and asset market Supply drivers
The supply of new space as shown previously in the theoretical framework is jointly determined by the replacement cost relative to asset prices, along with the cost of capital. Wheaton and Torto (1990) have highlighted the importance of the cost of capital in influencing industrial real estate demand, and have incorporated the long-term corporate AAA rated bonds with expected inflation based on a four-period average lag of current and past inflation. Also, current vacancy rates, a result of demand and supply conditions in the real estate market are likely to inform developers whether to bring in more supply or to hold off. The effect of construction cost on new supply has gotten mixed views in the literature, while some studies find it to be a significant explanatory factor (Sing, 2003; R. Thompson & Tsolacos, 2000). Others do not find it to be important determinant

(Barras & Ferguson, 1987). In our paper we use the construction cost index (CC), prime lending rates (PLR) and the 10-year government Treasury bond (T-Bond) yields as proxies representing the replacement costs of adding new supply into the strategic industrial real estate market.

In theory and if the strategic industrial real estate market is efficient and in equilibrium, all macroeconomic conditions affecting demand and supply would be fully reflected in prices that would determine the amount of new supply in the future (DiPasquale & Wheaton, 1996). However, real estate markets often do not instantaneously adjust to information unlike the common stock markets and often exhibits long term forward looking behaviour. The composite leading indicator although not a direct indicator of supply (CLI) anticipates turning point in economic growth cycles[xxxi] and can be important to explain decisions taken by developers on whether to build or to postpone development. Despite the limitations of having most of the earlier econometric empirical studies revolving around the Northern American and European markets, Sing (2003) enhanced the econometric empirical studies on Singapore's industrial landscape by formulating a VECM to explain the dynamic relationship between the private industrial space demand and other property related demand and supply determinants, using Singapore's private industrial property market data.

Chow *et al.* (2002) in their analysis of the Singapore industrial real estate (1989-2000) market observed that new space supply responds negatively to vacancy rates and financing cost (interest rates)[xxxii] but positively to capital values. An interesting claim in their study was that the supply of industrial space in Singapore during the study period seemed to have moved from a firm centred decision to a profit oriented investment class. This behaviour of the strategic industrial real estate market as an asset class in Singapore has only increased over the past several years with the introduction of new strata titled industrial properties[xxxiii].

Previous studies have used methodologies such as single equation OLS (ordinary least squares), simultaneous system of equations approach to discover the dynamic interactions of various economic variables concerned with the strategic industrial real estate market. Sims (1980) however commends the use of VAR models in econometric modelling, due to previous criticisms of constraints imposed by economic theory on the more traditional economic models based on ordinary OLS or simultaneous equation systems (Thompson & Tsolacos, 2000). When used wisely, VARs based on economic reasoning can both fit the data and provide sensible estimates of the casual relationship between related variables (Stock & Watson, 2001). We expected to find co-integrating vectors due to inherent long run relationships observed in previous studies in Singapore (Chow *et al.*, 2002; Sing, 2003). However, our Johnasen's co-integration tests did not find any for our selected variables, possibly due to the short time span under study. In accordance with our literature review, the generic VAR model consists of six endogenous variables and three exogenous macroeconomic variables, giving us a set of six empirical specifications that holistically models the strategic industrial real estate market in Singapore. Our structural VAR model that captures the space, asset and development market for strategic industrial real estate market is given by Eq. (4):

$$Y_i = f(NABS, GDP, PPI, CR, VC, CC, CLI, PLR, TB) \qquad (4)$$

, where

NABIS = Net absorption of industrial space,
GDP = Absolute contributions to Gross Domestic Product from the manufacturing and R&D sector,
PPI = Overall industrial property price index,
CR = Market wide industrial capitalization rate,
VC = Island wide industrial vacancy rates
CC = Construction cost index,
CLI * = Composite Leading Indicator (CLI),
PLR = Prime lending rate,
TB * = Government T-Bond yield.
*exogenously specified into the VAR

The prime lending rate, Composite leading indicator and T-bond yield are *exogenous* variables that represent the development market in our model. This is because we believe these variables are not directly involved in the dynamics of the space and asset markets in Singapore[xxxiv] but act as external factors, which determine decisions about timing in the development sector.

The Data

We utilize a 10-year quarterly time series data provided by Real Estate Information System (*REALIS, URA*) for our selected variables. Although the time period is not too long (38 observations), during this time period there has been three cycles in Singapore as indicated by the industrial property price index in Figure 3. We believe this time period captures sufficient dynamics of the strategic industrial real estate market in Singapore. Economic variables like the manufacturing gross domestic product[xxxv], the composite leading indicator (CLI), prime lending rate (PLR) and Government treasury 10-year bond yields were obtained from *DATASTREAM* subscribed by the National University of Singapore.

Figure 3. Quarterly time series of Singapore's Industrial property price index

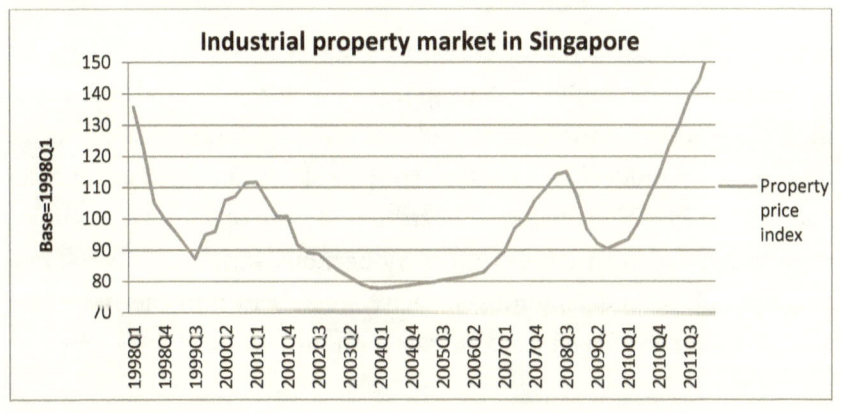

Source: REALIS, 2012

KIM HIN DAVID HO

Variables were converted into their log forms for ease of interpretation, and since all the variables were integrated of order one I(1), and subsequently differenced before adopting the Vector autoregressive (VAR) model. Also, we do not find the set of chosen variables to co-integrate over time, rejecting the use of a vector error correction model. Descriptive statistics of the concerned variables are given in Table 1.

Table 1: Descriptive statistics

	LCLI	LCR	LGDP	LNABS	LPLR	LPPI	LTB	LCC	LVC
Mean	4.602188	1.511619	4.120496	12.12739	1.690673	4.527374	3.153111	4.638030	2.528951
Median	4.596129	1.696999	4.130161	12.35390	1.677097	4.521789	3.140000	4.606170	2.517696
Maximum	4.783316	1.915309	4.249621	13.06017	1.766442	4.744932	4.670000	4.951593	2.992393
Minimum	4.422449	0.797008	3.980669	9.350189	1.667707	4.355426	1.990000	4.455509	1.897120
Std. Dev.	0.103953	0.391483	0.086435	0.711973	0.033870	0.127855	0.729414	0.143822	0.273058
Skewness	0.068677	-0.861253	-0.110552	-1.693874	1.543773	0.188162	0.338022	0.565724	-0.242080
Kurtosis	1.890275	1.991307	1.536449	6.757524	3.625175	1.670083	2.321168	2.269153	2.734573
Jarque-Bera	2.344417	7.470915	4.107879	47.99218	18.60710	3.581808	1.720965	3.401837	0.571617
Probability	0.309682	0.023862	0.128229	0.000000	0.000091	0.166809	0.422958	0.182516	0.751407
Sum	207.0985	68.02284	185.4223	545.7324	76.08027	203.7318	141.8900	208.7114	113.8028
Sum Sq. Dev.	0.475470	6.743401	0.328726	22.30382	0.050476	0.719263	23.40996	0.910126	3.280666
Observations	45	45	45	45	45	45	45	45	45

The VAR Model Estimation

From the above selected variables, we construct our empirical model to predict the dynamics of Singapore's strategic industrial real estate market. The estimation is carried out using an unrestricted vector autoregressive model (VAR), which consists of five endogenous variables and three exogenous variables. The structural form of the VAR equations to be estimated with its respective endogenous variables is as follows, and for ease of understanding we have split them into the space and asset market equations in accordance with our theoretical framework.

Space market

$$\Delta \text{LNABS}_t = \mu_t + \sum \alpha_0 \Delta \text{LGDP}_{t-1} + \sum \alpha_1 \Delta \text{LCC}_{t-1} + \sum \alpha_2 \Delta \text{LVC}_{t-1} +$$
$$\sum \alpha_3 \Delta \text{PPI}_{t-1} + \sum \alpha_4 \Delta \text{LNABS}_{t-1} + \sum \alpha_5 \Delta \text{LCap}_{t-1} + \alpha_6 \Delta \text{LTB}_t +$$
$$\alpha_7 \Delta \text{LCLI}_t + \alpha_8 \Delta \text{LPLR}_t + \varepsilon_{0t} \qquad (5)$$

$$\Delta \text{CC}_t = \mu_1 + \sum \beta_0 \Delta \text{LGDP}_{t-1} + \sum \beta_1 \Delta \text{LCC}_{t-1} + \sum \beta_2 \Delta \text{LVC} + \sum \beta_3 \Delta \text{LPPI}_{t-1}$$
$$+ \sum \beta_4 \Delta \text{LNABS}_{t-1} + \sum \beta_6 \Delta \text{LCap}_{t-1} + \beta_7 \text{LCLI}_t + \beta_7 \Delta \text{LTB}_t +$$
$$\beta_8 \Delta \text{LPLR}_t + \varepsilon_{0t} \qquad (6)$$

$$\Delta \text{GDP}_t = \mu_t + \sum \gamma_0 \Delta \text{LGDP}_{t-1} + \sum \gamma_1 \Delta \text{LCC}_{t-1} + \sum \gamma_2 \Delta \text{LVC}_{t-1} +$$
$$\sum \gamma_3 \Delta \text{PPI}_{t-1} + \sum \gamma_4 \Delta \text{LNABS}_{t-1} + \sum \gamma_5 \Delta \text{LCap}_{t-1} + \gamma_6 \Delta \text{LTB}_t +$$
$$\gamma_7 \Delta \text{LCLI}_t + \gamma_8 \Delta \text{LPLR}_t + \varepsilon_{0t} \qquad (7)$$

Asset market

$$\Delta \text{CAP}_t = \mu_t + \sum \zeta_0 \Delta \text{LGDP}_{t-1} + \sum \zeta_1 \Delta \text{LCC}_{t-1} + \sum \zeta_2 \Delta \text{LVC}_{t-1} +$$
$$\sum \zeta_3 \Delta \text{PPI}_{t-1} + \sum \zeta_4 \Delta \text{LNABS}_{t-1} + \sum \zeta_5 \Delta \text{LCap}_{t-1} + \zeta_6 \Delta \text{LTB}_t +$$
$$\zeta_0 \Delta \text{LCLI}_t + \zeta_0 \Delta \text{LPLR}_t + \varepsilon_{0t} \qquad (8)$$

$$\Delta \text{PPI}_t = \mu_t + \sum \xi_0 \Delta \text{LGDP}_{t-1} + \sum \xi_1 \Delta \text{LCC}_{t-1} + \sum \xi_2 \Delta \text{LVC}_{t-1} +$$
$$\sum \xi_3 \Delta \text{PPI}_{t-1} + \sum \xi_4 \Delta \text{LNABS}_{t-1} + \sum \xi_5 \Delta \text{LCap}_{t-1} +$$
$$\xi_6 \Delta \text{LTB}_t + \xi_0 \Delta \text{LCLI}_t + \xi_0 \Delta \text{LPLR}_t + \varepsilon_{0t} \qquad (9)$$

$$\Delta \text{VC}_t = \mu_t + \sum \kappa_0 \Delta \text{LGDP}_{t-1} + \sum \kappa_1 \Delta \text{LCC}_{t-1} + \sum \kappa_2 \Delta \text{LVC}_{t-1} +$$
$$\sum \kappa_3 \Delta \text{PPI}_{t-1} + \sum \kappa_4 \Delta \text{LNABS}_{t-1} + \sum \kappa_5 \Delta \text{LCap}_{t-1} +$$
$$\kappa_6 \Delta \text{LTB}_t + \kappa_0 \Delta \text{LCLI}_t + \kappa_0 \Delta \text{LPLR}_t + \varepsilon_{0t} \qquad (10)$$

The six equations together form the complete system of dynamic equations where α's, β's, γ's, ζ's, ξ's and κ's are the structural parameters of each endogenous variable, which when estimated are believed to represent the complete behavioural structure of the Singapore strategic industrial real estate market. The reduced form p-th order VAR represented in Eq (4), can be denoted by VAR (p) and represented as follows,

$$Y_i = \mu + A_1 y_{t-1} + A_2 y_{t-2} \ldots \ldots + A_n y_{t-p} + e_t \qquad (11)$$

Where μ is a K×1 vector of constants representing intercepts, A_i is a K×K matrix of with lags p. The error term e_t is a $k \times 1$ vector of error terms that satisfies all three assumptions of a vector autoregressive equation (zero mean, no serial correlation and a contemporaneous covariance matrix). The above VAR specification was subjected to two lags, the lag order selection criteria function is based on various independent statistics and showed three lags to be optimal. However, this was reduced to two lags in order to minimize serial autocorrelations exhibited by the prior model. As mentioned previously, the Johansen Co-integration tests results were futile, leading to the notion that the variables selected did not exhibit long run equilibrium at least within our chosen time span.

The Estimation results

First, we look at the weighted least square regression (WLS)[xxxvi] coefficients for our estimated equations (5)-(10) of Table 2. Our variables of interest would be the net absorption and industrial property price index that would adequately capture both the space and asset market behaviour over time. The net space absorption is highly volatile and hence a one percentage positive change in previous period leads to a revision of 0.91% percentage points downwards in the current period. Similarly, a one percentage change in the cap rate by one quarter in the past reduces space absorption by 3%. This is consistent with theory, i.e. a positive change in cap rate would entail an increase in rentals to capital value ratio, which in turn could add to downward pressure on demand for space. A simple granger causality test at two lags confirms this one directional casualty[xxxvii].

An increase in GDP that includes manufacturing output and R&D expenditure, both set to create new demand for expansionary activities, have a positive impact on space absorption as expected. A one percentage positive change of GDP in the previous quarter increases net absorption by 5.94%, and this is statistically significant at the 5 percent level. However, simple granger causality tests between these two variables do not show causality between GDP and net space absorption and vice-versa, hinting a third channel for an observed effect on space absorption.

A one percentage increase in net absorption two quarters in the past increased the property price index by a very small percentage (0.001%). The best predictor was its own lagged variables where a one percentage increase in the past (two quarters) is followed by 0.76% increase in the present, a behaviour due to serial correlation behaviour exhibited by the index. Construction costs and the composite leading indicator also seem to have an impact on the property price index, all of which are rather intuitive. The effect of interest rates on net absorption is found to be insignificant. This can be due to less dependence of industrial expansionary activities on domestic capital. For example, in 2005 the manufacturing industry stood second (33.3%) to financial services (38.3%) in absorbing foreign direct investments (FDI) in Singapore[xxxviii]. Also, an increase in property price indices in the past affect present vacancy strongly in a negative manner, possibly reflecting the investment nature of industrial properties previously observed in Singapore (Chow *et al.*, 2002).

The model seems robust in explaining these trends with the correct specification being selected, based on Akaike and Schwarz criterion. The model is also free from serial and autocorrelation issues, which make the coefficients unbiased and robust. The normality tests concluded that the residuals were normally distributed. However good the structural coefficients are in a VAR model, we always need to be careful about their casual interpretation as time aggregation, the omission of variables and random shocks may distort direct policy conclusions (Canova, 2011). For this reason we carry out impulse response functions along with variance decomposition analysis for more reliable insights of the results.

The Impulse response and variance decomposition analysis

Vector auto regression (VAR) methods have a unique advantage over other econometric analysis in that the analysis need not conform to economic theory (Sims, 1980). However, a structural VAR can use economic theory to sort out the links between variables through time albeit with the help of institutional knowledge about the system under study (Blanchard & Watson, 1986; Sims, 1986). Our structural VAR in the previous section was used to make casual interpretations using the four quadrant theoretical framework that explain the real estate dynamics using the variables involved. Although the above causality model is insightful for policy makers, there could be other hidden variables in the macroeconomic structure that might change, thereby making it difficult to draw concrete inferences on the behaviour of interdependent time series variables. Thus, structural inferences and policy analysis become difficult since they require differentiating correlation with causality.

Table 2. Vector auto regression model estimation using Weighted Least Squares (WLS)

Dependent variables	Δ LNABS$_t$	Δ LCR$_t$	Δ PPI$_t$	Δ VC$_t$	Δ GDP$_t$	Δ CC$_t$
Constant	0.037	0.04*	-0.004	0.009	0.003	-0.005
Δ LNABS$_{t-1}$	-0.91***	-0.04	-0.005	-0.01	-0.02**	0.005
Δ LNABS$_{t-2}$	-0.33**	0.06*	0.001*	-0.01	-0.005	0.20*
Δ CR$_{t-1}$	-3.07***	-0.06	-0.03	0.09	-0.02	0.06**
Δ CR$_{t-2}$	-1.5*	-0.40*	-0.04	-0.06	-0.06	0.01
Δ PPI$_{t-1}$	-2.5	-01.08	0.33**	-0.78**	0.07	0.21*
ΔPPI$_{t-2}$	-2.27	-1.04*	0.76***	-0.28	-0.13	0.09
Δ VC$_{t-1}$	0.83	-0.04	-0.03	0.09	-0.06	-0.03

ΔVC_{t-2}	1.32	-0.73**	-0.05	0.13	0.05	-0.02
ΔGDP_{t-1}	5.94**	0.15	0.15	0.29	-0.18	0.20*
ΔGDP_{t-2}	4.06	0.52	0.37	-0.02	-0.37	0.10
ΔCC_{t-1}	9.2	0.78	0.57**	0.67	0.16	0.39*
ΔCC_{t-2}	2.18	1.47*	-0.60	-1.65***	0.07	-0.02
$\Delta_{CLI(t)}$	0.04	-0.02**	0.007**	-0.004	0.006**	0.004**
$\Delta_{T\text{-Bond yield}(t)}$	0.16	0.06	-0.006	-0.013	0.007	-0.007
$\Delta_{PLR(t)}$	7.16	-1.59	0.03	1.59	0.87*	-0.73**

Adj. R-squared	0.62	0.06	0.66	0.36	0.3	0.42
S.E. of regression	0.5442	0.1437	0.0262	0.0721	0.0306	0.4252
Durbin-Watson stat	2,13	1.59	1.89	2.07	1.87	2.15

*,** and *** denote that coefficient is significant at 10%, 5% and 1% level respectively.

This would be the classical identification problem in econometrics, a problem which is hard to solve using statistics but usually mitigated with institutional knowledge about the subject in study (Stock and Watson, 2001). The most powerful function of VAR models lies in its ability to forecast and observe multivariate relationships between contemporaneously correlated time series. Vector auto regression models such as one performed in this paper offer an alternative to structural casual models where inter-temporal optimizing behaviour of individuals and firms are not captured (Lucas & Sargent, 1981; Sims, 1980). The two tools which illustrate such dynamics are the *impulse response* and *variance decomposition analysis*. The impulse response function traces the response of endogenous variable to change in one of the innovations (error term) in the system of equations.

As noted by previous authors, the ordering of variables is important. We use the conventional cholesky-dof adjusted decomposition to convert the structural VAR model into a recursive system for evaluation. We only report three specific impulse response functions such as for net absorption, property price index and vacancy rates. We believe they would capture essential aspects of asset and space market behaviour. Figure 4 shows the combined impulse response function (IRF) of other endogenous variables on net absorption. Our results show that a one standard deviation positive shock to the GDP increases the response of net absorption in the short to medium term (albeit lesser in magnitude). This is consistent with theory that expansionary activity leads to a positive effect on space absorption rates in Singapore.

Figure 4. Accumulated Responses of Net Absorption (LNABS) To Cholesky One S.D Innovations

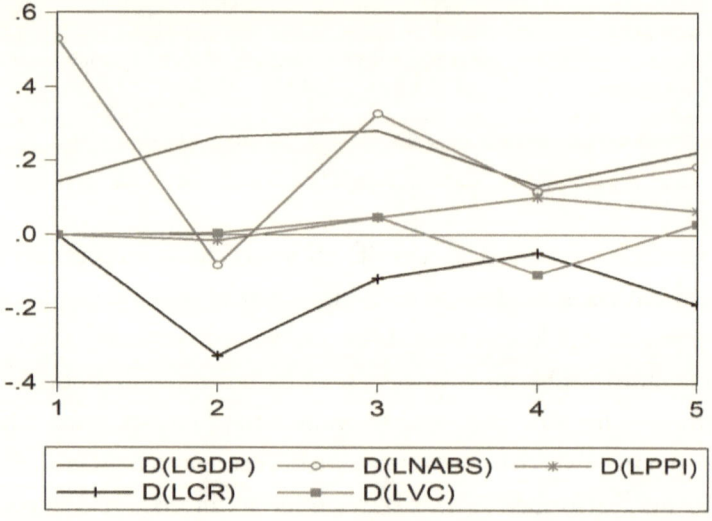

The effect of shocks to vacancy is positive on the space absorption behaviour in Singapore, possibly due to lower rental yields. On the asset side, we can look at the behaviour of cap rates (LCR) that captures rental yields and capital values. A one standard deviation positive shock to the cap rate (LCR) decreases net absorption in the short to medium term (Figure 5). This is expected as increases in the short term are mainly due to increasing rental yields that might deter immediate space absorption.

Figure 5. Accumulated Response of Capitalization Rates (LCR) To Cholesky One S.D Innovations

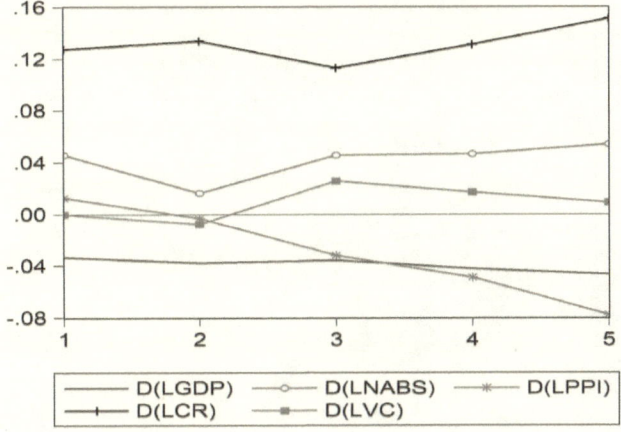

As shown by DiPasquale and Wheaton (1996)'s theoretical framework and explained in Section 2, an increase in space absorption would lead to a similar increase in market capitalization rates through increases in rental yields while keeping supply fixed in the short run. Similarly in the case of Singapore's strategic industrial real estate market, a one standard deviation positive shock to net absorption has a positive effect on cap rates (~4%) in the short to medium term. A similar shock to the property price index which represents capital values has a negative effect on the market cap values (LCR). This again is expected, as increases in capital values (LPPI) while keeping rental yields constant would bring down the overall cap rate[xxxix]. Shocks to GDP, does not exhibit positive behaviour of the cap rates as expected through the indirect channel of space absorption.

Moving over to the supply side behaviour, the vacancy of industrial real estate stock is enhanced by positive shocks given to the property price index, net absorption and GDP, all of which indicate expansionary activities that could potentially reduce vacancy rates in general (Figure 6). An interesting result shown in Figure 6 is that a one standard deviation positive shock given to cap rates[xl] increases vacancy rates in the short term, but reverting to negative over the medium term.

Figure 6. Accumulated Response of Vacancy Rates (LVC) To Cholesky One S.D Innovations

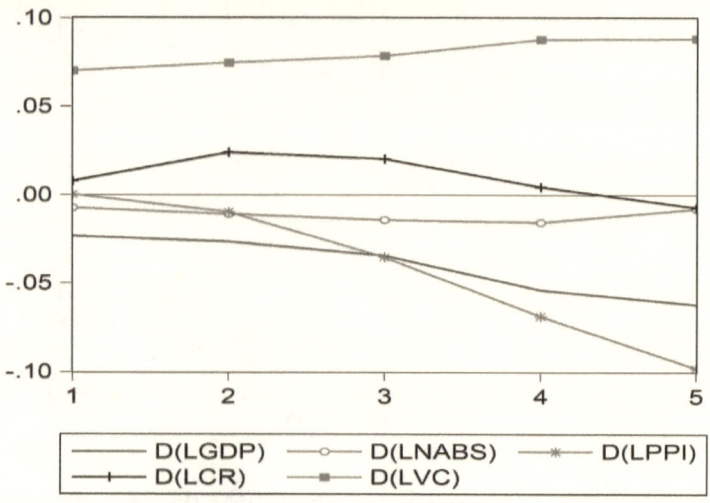

This behaviour could be due to the sensitivity of vacancy rates to rental yield movements in the short term. During our sample period (Figure 7) we find that the rental yields and vacancy rates in Singapore are highly negatively correlated (-0.65%). This possibly reflects the sensitivity of vacancy rates to rental yields and hence cap rates.

Figure 7. Island-wide industrial rental yields (LR) and vacancy rates (LVC) in Singapore

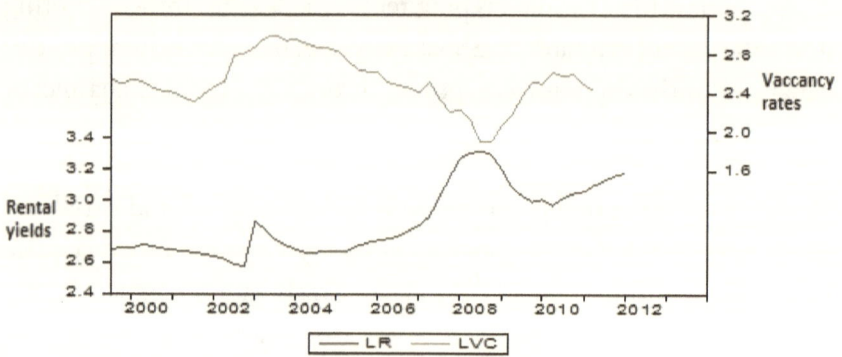

Source: REALIS, 2012

The Variance decomposition Analysis

Variance decomposition analysis shows the impact of one variable relative to other variables when given a random innovation shock to the entire VAR system. We are be able to determine how much of a change in a particular variable is due to its own shock and how much due to shocks in other variables in the system. We report three important variables, namely net space absorption (LNABS), cap rates (LCLI) and vacancy rates (LVC), to capture the essential dynamics of the strategic industrial real estate market in Singapore. Figure 8 shows the decomposition of variances for net absorption, GDP, property price index, cap rates following an initial shock (one S.E) to the net absorption (-12,050 sq. m) innovations. The space absorption (LNABS) accounted for the majority of its own variances throughout most of the period. However, by the end of the tenth period the effect of cap rate (14.11%), GDP (5.35%), vacancy rates (3.75%) did contribute to the variation in net absorption.

Figure 8. Generalized Forecast Error Variance Decomposition for the Variable LNABS

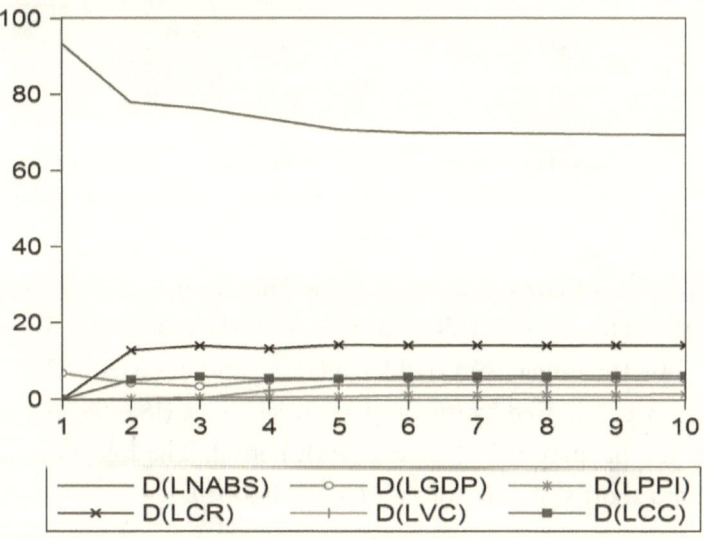

As shown in Figure 9 and given the same ordering of variables, the generalized forecast error variance decomposition arising from a one-standard error (S.E.) shock to vacancy rates, shows a self-inflicted variation up until the 8th period (35.3%). By the tenth period, the impact of property price index (36.12%) dominates variations in vacancy rates followed by construction costs (15.2%), GDP (7.62), and cap rates (5.19), all contributing to the variation of island wide industrial vacancy rates in Singapore.

Figure 9. Generalized Forecast Error Variance Decomposition for the Variable LVC

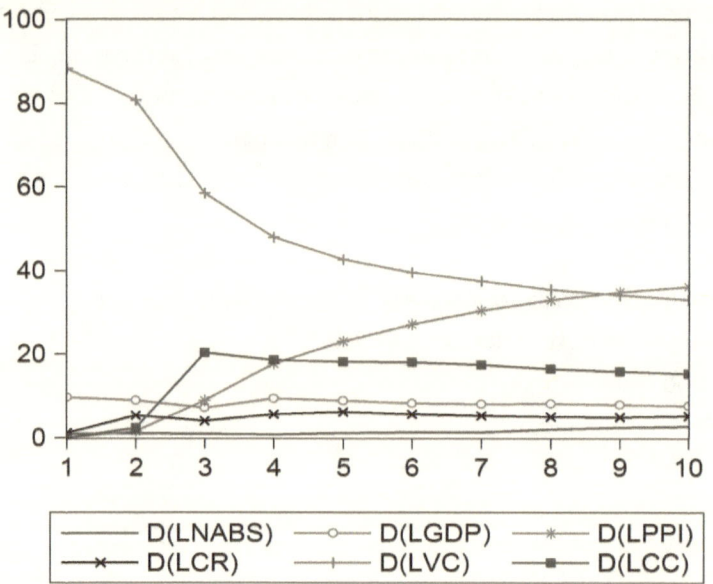

Similarly, the variance decomposition arising from a one-standard error (S.E.) shock to cap rates (~20 basis points) in the first period, is given in Table 3 by the impact of variables such as cap rates itself (82.8%) and GDP (5.6%) followed by the property price index (18.4 %) and the net absorption of space (13%) by the tenth period. The following section presents a short summary of the results obtained.

Table 3. Variance decomposition of cap rates

Period	S.E.	D(LNABS)	D(LGDP)	D(LPPI)	D(LCR)	D(LVC)	D(LCC)
1	0.140143	10.69489	5.634189	0.819225	82.85169	0.000000	0.000000
2	0.146692	13.79422	5.234539	1.896004	75.80608	0.273851	2.995314
3	0.158786	15.15764	4.486783	4.958746	66.39306	4.689906	4.313862
4	0.161592	14.63945	4.501742	5.868087	65.34718	4.821795	4.821747
5	0.166877	13.92375	4.293330	8.523333	62.72163	4.750875	5.787089
6	0.170738	13.49581	4.981197	11.53593	59.91703	4.538911	5.531122
7	0.174575	13.34919	4.974960	14.48421	57.37867	4.346086	5.466886
8	0.177778	13.36139	4.798347	16.43699	55.77483	4.355224	5.273219
9	0.181059	13.00517	4.781003	18.47575	54.20126	4.452474	5.084355
10	0.184548	13.02078	4.940568	20.53172	52.24393	4.320022	4.942983

Summary of key results

In looking at some of the results obtained, we can compare our findings with respect to the four quadrant theoretical model proposed by DiPasquale and Wheaton (1996) to see how the behaviour of Singapore's industrial market is shaped. Starting from the space market side of the strategic industrial real estate market we see that the current demand for new space is mainly driven by increase in manufacturing output as well as R&D expenditure in previous periods. A one percentage point increase in GDP in the previous quarter increases net space absorption by 5.3% in the current period. The generalized forecast error variance decomposition also shows that one-standard deviation shocks to the net space absorption (LNABS) over a ten period time frame accounts for an average of 73% of self-inflicted variance, with 13.5% due to market wide capitalization rates and 5.35% due to GDP variances and finally vacancy amounting to a mere 3.75%.

This result contradicts with an earlier finding in the private strategic industrial real estate market in Singapore where Sing (2003) finds a negative relationship between manufacturing GDP and private space demand of industrial properties. Sing attributes that this change could be due to three reasons, first it could be due to the firm's nature of non-substitution of space (i.e. capital intensive) in the face of increased production. Secondly and because Singapore is very land constrained, firms may take more space than they need and such a behaviour would reveal a 'disconnect' in observed market trends. Thirdly, firms may switch between private and public sector space providers. This behaviour could fail to reflect direct connection between GDP and space demand as the author's dataset is confined to the private strategic industrial real estate market. In our paper, we use both private and public real estate market data to show that the relationship is consistent with findings with empirical studies undertaken in the U.K (Giussani & Tsolacos, 1994; Nicholson & Tebbutt, 1979; Tsolacos, 1995) and in the U.S (William C. Wheaton & Torto, 1990).

On the asset side, cap rates (LCR) are positively influenced by changes in net absorption[xli] while negatively by capital values (LPPI) and vacancy rates (LVC)[xlii]. Similarly, better economic outlook given by the Composite leading indicator (LCLI) shows a negative impact on cap rates, possibly due to increasing positive expectations of capital values during those time periods. High rates of net absorption, strong property prices along with economic growth given by rising GDP all have a small albeit positive effect on cost of construction (LCC). Some studies have also related location specific factors affecting industrial rents and capital values in larger markets (Ambrose, 1990; Fehribach, Rutherford, & Eakin, 1993). However, as Singapore is relatively a small country we do not expect such spatial variations.

Concluding Comments

The academic literature on the dynamics of the Strategic industrial real estate market with some notable exceptions (Kling & McCue, 2002; R. Thompson & Tsolacos, 2000; William C. Wheaton & Torto, 1990) are still scarce when compared to its counterparts such as the housing and office markets (Capozza *et al.*, 2002; Case & Shiller, 1989; Glaeser & Gyourko, 2006; Mankiw & Weil, 1989; Quigley, 1999). The objective of our paper is to understand the fundamental structure and behaviour of the industrial real estate in Singapore, and to broadly indicate the relative impacts of macroeconomic conditions on real estate market dynamics.

We acknowledge that the structure and function of Industrial real estate especially in developed economies are fundamentally changing, moving away from a traditional factory type model to more adaptable spaces that accommodate the creative and knowledge intensive industrial activities. These high-technology facilities have the potential to create more attractive and integrated work spaces that have high investment value. Thus, an understanding of their underlying factors would be useful for academicians, investors and policy makers. In this paper and for the case of Singapore, we adopt the unrestricted vector autoregressive (VAR) approach to understand how the space and asset markets in industrial real estate are shaped through endogenous and exogenous factors. In Singapore, we find evidence for such a market to follow most of the theoretical predictions of the four quadrant model of real estate dynamics proposed by DiPasquale and Wheaton (1999). The resulting model is robust and the results are intuitive as well as insightful for academicians and public policy makers to understand the behaviour of the strategic industrial real estate market in Singapore.

(The author wishes to acknowledge his appreciation to Dr Rengarajan Satyanarain, *a former NUS research scholar, and presently a management information system consultant; for his dynamic perseverance and contribution in sourcing* the related literature, *the required primary and secondary data and treatment, and for the initial analysis).*

References

Ambrose, B. W. (1990). An analysis of the factors affecting light industrial property valuation. *Journal of Real Estate Research, 5*(3), 355-370.

Atteberry, W. L., & Rutherford, R. C. (1993). Industrial real estate prices and market efficiency. *Journal of Real Estate Research, 8*(3), 377-385.

Barras, R., & Ferguson, D. (1987). Dynamic modelling of the building cycle: 2. Empirical results. *Environment and Planning A, 19*(4), 493-520.

Blanchard, O. J., & Watson, M. W. (1986). Are business cycles all alike? *The American business cycle: Continuity and change* (pp. 123-180): University of Chicago Press.

Canova, F. (2011). *Methods for applied macroeconomic research* (Vol. 13): Princeton University Press.

Capozza, D. R., Hendershott, P. H., Mack, C., & Mayer, C. J. (2002). Determinants of real house price dynamics: National Bureau of Economic Research.

Case, K. E., & Shiller, R. J. (1989). The efficiency of the market for single-family homes: National Bureau of Economic Research Cambridge, Mass., USA.

Chow, Y. L., Ong, S. E., & Thang, D. C.-L. (2002). A cointegration approach to understanding Singapore's industrial space supply. *Journal of Property Investment & Finance, 20*(2), 96-115.

DiPasquale, D., & Wheaton, W. C. (1996). Urban economics and real estate markets. *New Jersey.*

Fehribach, F. A., Rutherford, R. C., & Eakin, M. E. (1993). An analysis of the determinants of industrial property valuation. *Journal of Real Estate Research, 8*(3), 365-376.

Giussani, B., & Tsolacos, S. (1994). Investment in industrial buildings: modelling the determinants of new orders. *Journal of Property Research, 11*(1), 1-15.

Glaeser, E. L., & Gyourko, J. (2006). Housing dynamics: National Bureau of Economic Research.

Kling, J. L., & McCue, T. E. (2002). Stylized facts about industrial property construction. *Journal of Real Estate Research, 6*(3), 293-304.

Lucas, R. E., & Sargent, T. (1981). After keynesian macroeconomics. *Rational expectations and econometric practice, 1*, 295-319.

Mankiw, N. G., & Weil, D. N. (1989). The baby boom, the baby bust, and the housing market. *Regional Science and Urban Economics, 19*(2), 235-258.

Nicholson, R., & Tebbutt, S. (1979). Modelling of new orders for private industrial building. *The Journal of Industrial Economics, 28*(2), 147-160.

Quigley, J. M. (1999). Real estate prices and economic cycles. *International Real Estate Review, 2*(1), 1-20.

Rabianski, J., & Black, R. T. (1997). Why Analysts Often Make Wrong Estimates Concerning the Demand For Industrial Space. *Real Estate Review, 27*, 68-72.

RICS. (1994). *Understanding the Property Cycle: Economic cycles and property cycles*: Royal Institution of Chartered Surveyors.

Sims, C. A. (1980). Macroeconomics and reality. *Econometrica: Journal of the Econometric Society*, 1-48.

Sims, C. A. (1986). Are forecasting models usable for policy analysis? *Federal Reserve Bank of Minneapolis Quarterly Review*, *10*(1), 2-16.

Sing, T. F. (2003). Dynamics of Private Industrial Space Demand in Singapore. *Journal of Real Estate Research*, *25*(3), 301-324.

Stock, J. H., & Watson, M. W. (2001). Vector autoregressions. *Journal of Economic perspectives*, 101-115.

Thompson, B., & Tsolacos, S. (1999). Rent adjustments and forecasts in the industrial market. *Journal of Real Estate Research*, *17*(2), 151-167.

Thompson, R., & Tsolacos, S. (2000). Projections in the industrial property market using a simultaneous equation system. *Journal of Real Estate Research*, *19*(2), 165-188.

Tsolacos, S. (1995). Industrial property development in the UK: a regional analysis of new orders. *Journal of Property Research*, *12*(2), 95-125.

Wheaton, W. C. (2003). Real estate "cycles": some fundamentals. *Real Estate Economics*, *27*(2), 209-230.

Wheaton, W. C., & Torto, R. G. (1990). An Investment Model of the Demand and Supply For Industrial Real Estate. *Real Estate Economics*, *18*(4), 530-547. doi: 10.1111/1540-6229.00536

Chapter 3

Urban Design and Planning Of The Knowledge Based Urban Development (KBUD) Under Agent Based Modelling (ABM)

The knowledge-based economy can be defined to be the major production and services centre, "based on knowledge-intensive activities that contribute to an accelerated pace of technological and scientific advancement, and rapid obsolescence" (Powell & Snellman, 2004, OECD, 2000). Industrialized nations, have undertaken large urban industrial real estate developments, known as the 'Knowledge Based Urban Development' (KBUD).[xliii] Knight, (1995) defines the transformation of knowledge resources into local development [that] could provide a basis for sustainable development'. From an economic view point, the KBUD can be defined as 'one in which economic growth is centred on the production, distribution and use of technology' (Bajracharya & Too, 2009). A more planning-oriented definition is that 'they [the KBUDs] are a cluster of research and development (R&D) activities, high-tech manufacturing of knowledge-intensive industrial and business sectors linked by the mixed-use environment including housing, business, education and leisure within an urban-like setting'

(Yigitcanlar *et al.*, 2008). The planning-oriented definition views the KBUD as a new planning paradigm in the knowledge-based society, in which the 'ultimate goal is for a city to be designed to encourage and enable the production and circulation of abstract work' (Cheng, Choi, Chen, Eldomiaty, & Millar, 2004). Combined with globally oriented consultancies and services, the resultant network helps to disseminate new knowledge between different actors (Gadrey, Gallouj & Weinstein, 1995; Hertog, 2000; Muller & Zenker, 2001a).

At the broader urban policy level to facilitate the KBUDs, the major goal is to adopt the 'triple helix model' of innovation by Etzkowitz and Leydesdorff (2000). Their model hypothesizes that the interaction among three key institutions: government, university and the private sector. The actors in the key institutions comprise the high technology firms; public, private and university research institutions; the polytechnics, the schools and the supporting Knowledge Intensive Business Services (KIBS) that help to bring about the 'system of innovation'.[xliv] The availability of a diversity of resources to learn enables the technology firms to better innovate. These firms interact with other firms and with other participants in the cluster like the universities, research institutes, suppliers and consumers. The result is 'interactive learning'Lundvall (1985). Several studies have documented rising improvements in the firms' innovative capability, when the firms interact with their participating actors (Cooke, 2001; Coombs, Narandren, & Richards, 1996; Freeman & Soete, 1997; Oerlemans, Meeus, & Boekema, 2001; Pavitt, Robson, & Townsend, 1987; Von Hippel, 1976) . Urban planning studies accorded due interest in post-industrial cluster development under the KBUD paradigm (Carrillo, 2004; Yigitcanlar, Velibeyoglu, & Martinez-Fernandez, 2008). Earlier KBUD studies advocated the social, institutional and cultural aspects that are imperative for the sustainable growth of planned clusters (Isaksen, 2004; Knight, 1995; Yigitcanlar, 2009). The literature has identified five broad themes that most knowledge-based developments strive to achieve (Yigitcanlar *et al.* (2008):

- living and working,
- centrality,
- connectivity,
- learning and playing, and
- branding.

The living and working theme for mixed-use developments denotes a central goal of the KBUD like the Helsinki Digital Village in Finland and the Kelvin Grove Urban Village in Brisbane while the learning and playing theme is an inherent part of the KBUD like the Copenhagen Crossroads and the Zaragoza Digital Mile in Spain. Connectivity to a global talent pool and the intra-cluster physical connectivity through pedestrian-oriented urban design, denotes the central goals of Singapore's One North industrial real estate research park development. The city branding or rebranding theme creates new symbolic value to old industrial cities (Bajracharya & Too, 2009). Such a theme includes the knowledge-based developments like the Taipei 101, the @22 Barcelona and the Seoul Digital Media City.

According to Searle and Pritchard (2008), the KBUDs can be divided into three types of clusters, based on what activity type they support. The first activity type includes the knowledge-intensive service cluster that houses corporate headquarters and the higher order business and financial services, i.e. the 'Financial City' model. The second activity type clusters specialized high-technology research and development (R&D) activities in fields like information and communications technology (ICT), the life sciences (biomedical and biotechnology) and the media industries (for e.g. Singapore's Biopolis industrial real estate research park, Maryland's DNA valley and Cambridge's Science Park). The third activity type hosts creative fields for cultural knowledge production like the arts, media and entertainment industries (for e.g. Seoul's Digital Media City, Media City UK, 22@Barcelona, and Gold Coast Cultural and Civic Precinct and Brisbane Kelvin Grove Urban Village). The literature focused on case studies that evaluate the institutional and governance aspects (Chatzkel, 2004; Garcia, 2004;

Isaksen, 2004; Knight, 1995; Yigitcanlar, 2009; Yigitcanlar, Metaxiotis, & Carrillo, 2012; Yigitcanlar, Velibeyoglu, et al., 2008). The literature is concerned with the development of institutional planning models and the identification of metrics that evaluate the performance of the knowledge-based developments. Various authors look at generalized institutional planning model approaches, which the planning authorities can adopt to create sustainable developments. Such model approaches include the KBUD Analysis Model (Yigitcanlar, 2008), the KBUD Characteristics Model (Van Winden et al, 2007), the KnowCis Model (Ergazakis et al., in 2006), the Alert Model (Corey and Wilson, 2006) and the famous MAKCi Model established by the World Capital Institute in 2006. There has been limited studies that look at effective urban design strategies.

Two gaps in the KBUD literature are worth exploring. First, few people[xlv] looked at the functional role possibility that physical design can play to induce or facilitate intra-cluster interactions of the KBUD real estate. Such intra-cluster interactions enable a vibrant and interactive local environment, a phenomenon known as the 'local buzz' (Asheim, Coenen, & Vang, 2007; Bathelt, Malmberg, & Maskell, 2004). Urban design is an important medium to bring the related actors closer on the ground for mutual benefit. Mixed-use zoning policies stipulate adjacent and overlapping land uses to separate compatible and incompatible land uses in cities via complementary zoning. Urban design strategies for knowledge-based clusters remain highly experimental. They tend focus on aesthetic attributes to create iconic and futuristic architectural landscapes.[xlvi] The land-use design role of facilitating spontaneous and planned interactions for knowledge-based clusters, remains as a major avenue that is less explored in the literature. Secondly, the static designs of long-term master plans are becoming an unfavorable option for the dynamic design of the KBUDs, wherein the inflow and outflow of people and businesses imply that the KBUD urban planning and design should take them into consideration. Long-term, predetermined 'zoning' plans, often a product of the underlying KBUD urban design, do not materialize on the ground owing to ever-changing market conditions (Abukhater, 2009; Torres, 2006). Urban design has been depicted to be a 'black box' in the urban development process, owing to the presence of subjective and often conflicting design goals of the planners and designers (Schlager, 1965). As a result, two study questions can be posed:

- What is an optimal urban design criterion[xlvii] for the KBUD that can potentially enhance intra-cluster knowledge interactions?
- How can the KBUD be dynamically[3] designed as the specialized large industrial real estate?

These questions pose important implications for urban planners and designers of knowledge-based clusters for creating vibrant, mixed-use specialized large industrial real estate. Chapter 3 comprises several sections with the first section providing the introduction. The next (second) section is concerned with the related literature on the KBUD's knowledge-based interactions of high-technology clusters, inclusive of its associated actors, on innovation and proximity dynamics. The third section looks at the knowledge interaction design criteria (KIDC), which in turn provides the KBUD land use design guidelines. The fourth section discusses the paper's methodology, the drawbacks of land use design models (LUDMs); the conceptual framework of the KBUD-land use design model (KBUD-LUDM) that adopts the agent based, large industrial real estate model approach; the model's data requirements; and the model itself as a meaningful KBUD design tool. The fifth section concludes the paper.

The Related Literature

The importance of knowledge in catalyzing the process of technological innovation is reiterated in the science and technology literature (Hargadon & Sutton, 1997; Kanter, 1988; Mascitelli, 2000; Nonaka & Konno, 1998). Individuals working in knowledge-intensive industries

---

3   or incrementally.

require information resources within their spatial horizon to facilitate the consumption of existing information. Face-to-face interaction among the individual workers is an important medium that facilitates the creation, sharing and transfer of knowledge. Such interaction denotes the consultations among peers that involve the task-related exchange of information. In her seminal work, Sonnenwald (1999) has shown that workers, exposed to a large number of information resources (like the mentors, the peers for consultation, the literature, and the subject experts), would expand their knowledge more than the unexposed groups of workers. Earlier studies highlighted the important face-to-face consultation of the knowledge-related workspaces. In his seminal analysis on R&D projects, Allen (1984) showed that an increase in the number of consultations among research groups would correlate with higher subjective expert ratings of R&D effectiveness. In studying team performance of an education department, Ancona and Caldwell (1992) has found that knowledge expansion would accrue from face-to-face worker interaction that benefitted overall team performance. Salter and Gann (2003) demonstrated that the non-routine patterns of work[xlviii] of the high technology workers, are dependent on the face-to-face peer interaction for problem solving and ideas transfer. Such studies provide a strong basis for enabling the design community to support the notion that there exists a potential contribution for work place planning, which essentially mold human behavior and interactions in the R&D-oriented environments (Toker & Gray, 2008). Design studies advocate the design of workspace that emphasizes the provision of informal spaces and social amenities, like the cafes, bars and restaurants that promote social interactions. Coupled with private spaces to support concentrated work, enables the formation of the creative environment via readily facilitating information exchange (Duffy, 1997; Duffy *et al.*, 2012).

Studies on the beneficial effects of design to sustain face-to-face interactions are limited for the microenvironment (for e.g. at the real estate asset level). There appears to be a lack of understanding regarding how design can benefit the large scale, knowledge-based developments. For the planned knowledge-based clusters, the influence of spatial design does not exist at the real estate asset level but beyond that at the urban precinct[xlix] level. Land use design becomes important that helps to shape the relative position of the workers in space. Once the land use design characteristics of the participating actors and the determinants of their interaction among the actors are understood, such information can be utilized to create efficient land use designs for KBUDs. By placing the related actors together, complementary land use designs can be created, and they support the interaction patterns of peers, within and across the scientific fields.

Urban design helps to make the connections between people, places, movement, and urban form.[l] Urban design is often conducted by zoning instruments, stipulating that adjacent or overlapping land uses are identified and separated into compatible and incompatible land uses in urban spaces. The urban designer's role is to identify the types of connections or interactions[li] among the actors and their determinants to enable various land uses to be arranged in space. When formulating design goals for the large KBUD, it is useful to rely on some basic principles of formulating the design criteria by Lynch and Rodwin (1958). They recognize that the goal formulation process for any city or real estate development project should enhance two important relationships in space:

- The relationship of men and objects that relate people and buildings in their functional role;
- The relationship of men and men that is concerned with an interpersonal relation, like that for constructing surroundings that maximize interpersonal communications.

The first relationship is concerned with generating functional goals with regard to the type of environment that is to be achieved by the design, for e.g. a historical town, a housing neighborhood or an industrial real estate development. Lynch and Rodwin (1958) reiterate that first relationship denotes the sensual interactions between men and objects (i.e. the industrial real estate assets). Such interactions include aesthetical and physiological goals, which are to be achieved by the design, for e.g. the Victorian architectural facades for old town renewal programs, or the futuristic designs of modern industrial real estate developments. The second relationship is concerned with the explicit need to understand the relationship among individuals belonging to the different functional buildings or economic activities. This relationship can be a simple spatial connection like the relationship between housing and schools or retail shopping, between business activity and the transportation corridor. This spatial connection can influence how people interact with each other, how they move around and how they use a place for different purposes.[lii] This second relationship is more relevant for designing interactive spaces and achieving efficient land use design.

The KBUD interactions are of a higher order. Land use design facilitates the interaction between related workers that exist through collaboration, say between the scientists of one organization (for e.g. a high technology software firm) with another (for e.g. a university department). Therefore, the KBUD's design needs to satisfy an important design objective to create a spatial distribution, wherein the nearby actors are more likely to interact and to benefit from positive externalities. There is very little guidance for urban planners and designers to be cognizant of the nature of the participating actors, their characteristics in terms of the type of work they are involved in and their interaction patterns with one another. Chapter 3 seeks to fill this short coming. First, the definition and the nature of the KBUD knowledge interactions are explored, to be followed by a short account of the participating actors together with their characteristics in terms of the types of work they perform. Secondly, four determinants of the knowledge interaction among the knowledge-based workers are identified from the innovation and proximity dynamics literature. Thirdly, a design criterion is proposed that would house actors in space to achieve maximum interaction. Departing from the linear programming approach that has dominated previous land use design models, an agent based model approach is adopted to facilitate the KBUD design process (Barber, 1976; Correia

& Madden, 1985; Janssen van Herwijnen, Stewart & Aerts, 2008; Schlager, 1965; Williams, ReVelle & Levin, 2004). .

Knowledge interactions (KIs) denote 'the continuous and dynamic interaction(s) between tacit and explicit knowledge that occur at the individual, group, organizational and inter-organizational levels, which lead to the creation or sharing or the transfer of knowledge and information' (Ikujirō Nonaka & Takeuchi, 1995). Recent studies on knowledge-based clusters have identified the various types and channels through which interactions occur among the actors involved in the innovation process. KIs can occur through inter-personal relationships (i.e. personal, professional and mixed ones) that are formed as a result of intra-cluster collaborations (for e.g. in contract research); human capital transfers (i.e. intra-cluster job transfers); major events (for e.g. conferences and trade fairs); field- and sector- based communities (for e.g. research based consortiums) via the sharing of capital resources (for e.g. public and private grants and expensive equipment); and the unplanned accidental encounters (Asheim *et al.*, 2007; Kesidou, Caniëls, & Romijn, 2009; Lawson & Lorenz, 1999; Meeus, Oerlemans, & Hage, 2004). Spatial proximity plays an important role to support the knowledge interactions (KIs) through the formation of inter-personal relationships (formal and informal ones) and planned or unplanned encounters. According to Foray (2005), the barriers to the interaction among the 'related actors',[liii] are most sensitive to the expansion of geographical distance.

Utilizing spatial and behavioral data collected from knowledge based companies, Rashid, Kampschroer and Zimring (2006) showed that spatial layouts consistently influence worker movements and their subsequent interactions. At the building level, spatial layout is important in facilitating 'useful' KIs. Some studies provide empirical evidence to show that the rising mean integration of an area of a building would increase integration among the workers, as evidenced by rising interactions' frequency (Hillier *et al.*, 1990; Penn & Hillier, 1992). By providing adequate amenities, opportunities can be created for knowledge workers to meet and interact. When such land-use deigns bring complementary or inter-dependent knowledge activities together through mixed use zoning, then the overall probability of useful interactions would improve. As the 'related' actors are brought close to one another through mixed use zoning strategies, the actors and workers can readily benefit from positive externalities through planned and spontaneous 'face-to-face' interactions.

There is limited discussion in the literature on classifying the 'actors' in terms of their KIs and their relation(s) to space. Different types of actors interact, share and transfer knowledge in different ways. For e.g. an engineer may require frequent interactions with his supervisor, as the engineer's job entails more of the 'learning-by-doing' in comparison to a biotechnologist, who acquires new knowledge through codified information, such as from journal articles and newspapers. The intuitive way to achieve high levels of interactions in land use design would be to mix a variety of uses and to simultaneously step up the overall density of the industrial real estate development. The average spatial proximity among the participants on site would be reduced accordingly. For the KIs to occur between any two agents (or two workers), the spatial proximity is just one factor among others (Boschma, 2005). Hence, there is the need to classify the KBUD actors.

Table 3.1 presents the KBUD classification of its actors. The classification defines the actors concerned and each actor's role specific to the KBUD. Every actor not only performs a unique function but would also reflect a possible interaction with one another. The first actor, i.e. the University, acts as the locus of knowledge generation in knowledge based clusters because universities are deemed to be the sources of new knowledge (Anselin, Varga, & Acs, 1997; Feldman, 1994; Saxenian, 1994). Knowledge diffusion from university research can occur through formal cooperation with firms; via the mobility of university graduates into firms; and via informal social interactions between employees and university researchers (Torre & Rallet, 2005; Vas, 2009). Studies found a significant and positive effect of the presence of universities in locations with higher start-up rates; R&D facilities; high technology production and human capital (Bania, Calkins, & Dalenberg, 1992; De Meyer, 1991; Nelson, 1986; Rees & Stafford, 1986). Anselin *et al.* (1997) reiterate the importance of university research, owing to 'the importance of basic university research in the stimulation of technological innovation and higher productivity (that) is derived from the public good nature of the research, and the resulting positive externalities to the private sector in the form of knowledge spillovers.

Public research institute (PRI) s' role in the innovation process is well documented, utilizing case studies that concentrate on the analysis of high technology clusters like Silicon Valley in the Austin and San Antonio Corridor, Route 128 in Boston, the Cambridge Science Park region and the Phoenix area in the UK (Hobday, 1988; Saxenian, 1996; Segal, Smilor *et al.*, 1988; Smilor *et al.*, 1987; Wigand, 1988). PRIs have several channels of achieving their role. PRIs are engaged in the codification of information; in the publishing of scientific materials in journals; in undertaking contract research with firms in the form of joint R&D projects; in providing consulting programs to organizations; and in the training of personnel from industry (Fritsch & Schwirten, 1999). Cooke, 2001; Cooke, Uranga, & Etxebarria, 1998), highlight face-to-face interactions to be the important channels of knowledge transfer; and that the geographic proximity of the PRIs and the private sector would form the crucial component of the regional innovation systems (RIS).

PRIs like the Brookings, Scripps and Carnegie Mellon institutes, the extra-university research arms like the Max Plank and Rockefeller institutes, non-governmental organizations (NGOs) like the WRI, Greenpeace and the Amnesty International NGOs[4], can create a group of actors that are involved in the innovation process through applied research. Most NGOs are established to conduct research that addresses socially pressing issues, for e.g. AIDS, tuberculosis, and dengue fever.

---

4   WRI, World Resources Institute.

They often conduct experimental research programs. Technology firms denote the locus of industrial production and denote the central agents for commercializing and distributing new technology. Innovation and output are associated with firm entry, networks and higher productivity growth (Acs & Audretsch, 1990; Elfring & Hulsink, 2003; *Smith et al., 2005*). Knowledge transfer among firms in the cluster that has the strong manufacturing and R&D core can readily benefit from the inherent geographic proximity (Baptista & Swann, 1998; Pavitt, 1987).

Table 3.1. Classification of Participants of the Knowledge Based Urban Development (KBUD) by Their Role in the Knowledge Based Economy

Participants	Role in the knowledge cluster
University	Primary driver of knowledge creation
Public Research Institute (PRI)	State-funded basic and applied research (civilian- and defense-related)
Private, extra-university research institutes, NGO research establishments	Promotes more niche, goal-oriented, socially pressing research programs, clinical trial–oriented experimental research programs
Technology firms	Commercializing innovation and product formation
Service companies (KIBS)	Often dubbed as the 'third pillar of the knowledge economy – talent agencies, IT, legal, finance (includes venture capitalists), real estate services, etc.

Source: Author, 2021)

The services sector plays a direct role in the innovation process and is known as the knowledge intensive business services (KIBS). Services firms denote those 'firms (that perform) mainly for other firms, encompassing highly (intellectual) and value (adding) services' (Muller & Zenker, 2001b). Such services firms are of two types:

- Traditional knowledge intensive business services (KIBS); and
- New technology, knowledge intensive business services (KIBS).

The services sector is referred to as the third pillar of the knowledge economy that support the traditional services like the IT (information technology), financial, legal, training, networking, building and the real estate services to primarily cater to the universities, the PRIs and the high technology companies. Examples of new technology, knowledge intensive business services (KIBS) include the telecommunication services, new technology training, new technologies design inclusive of precision engineering, technical engineering and R&D consultancy services (den Hertog, 2002; Hertog, 2000).

Industrial clustering are ordered on three spatial scales to achieve the agglomeration economies Marshall (1920). Such clustering occurs at the regional, metropolitan and neighborhood levels.[liv] The geographic agglomeration of economic activities is strengthened, owing to falling transportation costs in moving goods, people and ideas. Studies have dealt with the beneficial effects of spatial proximity that enhance the processes of interactive learning and innovation. Spatial proximity facilitates trustful relationships, easy observations and immediate comparison through face-to-face interactions (Malmberg & Maskell, 2006). The KBUD localizes learning through reducing the cost or barrier of transferring ideas and information via knowledge interactions (KIs). Table 3.1's KIs are concerned with face-to-face communication among members of the 'innovation milieu' that denotes the knowledge-based workers from the state, academia and the private sector. The importance of KIs to facilitate innovation is well documented in the innovative milieu and in the knowledge spill over literature (Bottazzi & Peri, 2003; Camagni, 1991) .

Generally, any actor[lv] that is involved in the interactive learning process is attributable to three types of knowledge bases, i.e. the analytical, synthetic and symbolic knowledge bases. Knowledge workers who derive their expertise from the analytical knowledge base are involved in pure scientific discovery to explore the 'natural world' (Asheim *et al.*, 2007; Moodysson, Coenen, & Asheim, 2008). Knowledge workers who derive their expertise from the synthetic knowledge base are involved in the design or construction of a product to attain a specific functional goal (Moodysson et al., 2008). Actors belonging to these two types of knowledge bases are engaged with their KIs in comparison to the 'information interactions'[lvi]. Figure 3.1 depicts the classification of KIs of the knowledge-based cluster.

Figure 3.1. Representation of Interactive Learning in the Knowledge Based Urban Development (KBUD) According to Their Knowledge Bases

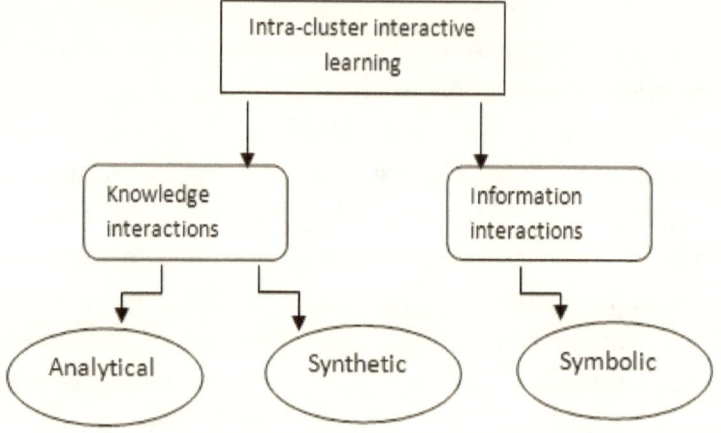

Source: Adapted from the classification by Asheim and Gertler (2005); Author, 2021

Information interactions are like the KIs but that the information interactions are confined to those interactions that occur among workers from industries that derive their expertise from the symbolic knowledge base. E.g.s of professions that belong to the symbolic knowledge base include architecture, the arts and craft, television and radio, advertising, publishing, the performing arts, gaming, design, fashion and the film and music industries. Such creative industries rely on skills acquired through 'learning by doing' in formal and informal settings. It is owing to their unique work nature, wherein the industrial real estate development projects require constant interaction on the basis of formal and informal communication 'along the way' (Asheim *et al*, 2007). The simplest way to enhance interaction levels through the urban design of a KBUD would be to zone all the actors according to the knowledge base, to which each actor belongs. This KBUD design type is depicted in Figure 3.2 that divides the KBUD site into specialized knowledge quadrants.

Figure 3.2. A Hypothetical Example of the Knowledge Based Urban Development (KBUD) Land Use Design Deploying Knowledge Bases as the Only Design Criteria

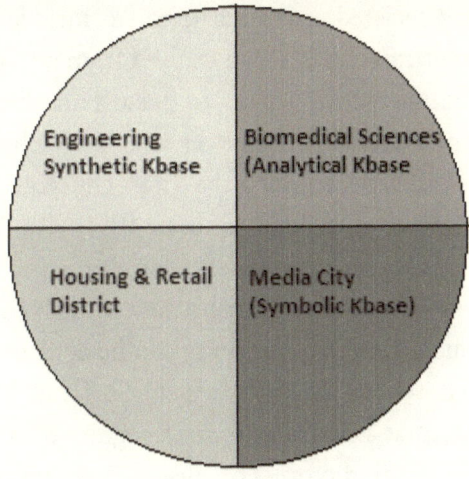

Source: Authors, 2021

An appropriate example of this KBUD type is Singapore's 'One North' industrial real estate research park, comprising knowledge specific zones for a biomedical hub, i.e. the Biopolis, a large engineering complex; the large sciences complex (i.e. the Fusionopolis) and the large media and arts district (i.e. the Mediapolis). The notion that geographic proximity is one of the most important criteria that fosters interactive learning among the knowledge workers, has been debunked by several authors (Asheim *et al.*, 2007; Boschma, 2005; Shaw & Gilly, 2000). The co-locating[lvii] of a diverse set of the actors concerned at the local or regional level is necessary but that it is not a sufficient condition to stimulate 'knowledge interactions' (KIs).

Boschma (2005) alludes proximity dynamics, which are required by the actors of the innovation process, to include the institutional, cognitive, social, organizational and geographical proximity aspects. He argues there is not just one but a confluence of all these proximity aspects that determine the probability of knowledge interactions (KIs) between any two agents or workers in space. Knowledge is often dispersed among the actors concerned, who in turn belong to different organizations. Actors in the knowledge economy denote the economic agents, who are subjected to bounded rationality[lviii]. The cognitive base is deemed to be any group that belongs to a particular field of science or an economic sector. Biomedical sciences have its associated economic sector to include the biomedical related technology firms. Knowledge transfer from one agent to another often requires the interacting agents to possess an absorptive capacity to identify, interpret and exploit new knowledge (Cohen & Levinthal, 1990). Cognitive differences among the actors concerned can constraint one another's absorptive capacity (Simon, 1955). Knowledge workers that belong to similar fields of science or similar economic sectors, should easily learn from one another because of their common domain expertise. Too much cognitive proximity can be detrimental to learning and innovation (Boschma, 2005; Pouder & St. John, 1996). Proximity among the actors that belong to similar cognitive bases may not be favorable to the innovation process because of three reasons.

First, the knowledge building process itself requires dissimilar and complementary bodies of knowledge to trigger new ideas and creativity. Secondly, too much cognitive proximity leads to the cognitive lock-in that denotes those routines within similar work-related networks, which can restrict new technologies or market opportunities. Such a lock-in leads to what is known as the 'competency trap' (Levitt & March, 1988). Thirdly, too much cognitive proximity increases the risk of involuntary knowledge spillovers, which prompt the competitors to be unwilling to share knowledge. Cantwell and Santangelo (2003) reiterate that the competing firms, who belong to similar scientific fields or economic sectors, do not co-locate their research activities to reduce the unintended spillovers.

Organizational practices are imperative to enable interactive learning (Boschma, 2005). Actors within similar organizations (be they small firms, large firms, academic departments and the polytechnics) are envisaged to share the reference and knowledge space that is bounded by an economic or a financial dependency. Such a proximity type can be divided into the intra-organizational proximity that refers to the internal management hierarchy (be it vertical or horizontal); and into the inter-organizational proximity that refers to the distance between two workers that belong to a similar organization. Similar organizational arrangements act like vehicles that enable knowledge and information exchange among the related agents (Cooke *et al.*, 1998).

Organizational proximity[lix] among the actors concerned is important to enable learning and innovation. Organizational proximity asserts strong control over new knowledge creation and ownership rights that also rewards its new technology efforts. Excessive proximity or too little proximity among the actors that belong to similar organizations can be a deterrent to learning and innovation. When there is too much inter-organizational proximity, the actors concerned are exposed to the risk of being accustomed to established relationships. As the search for novelty often requires the actors concerned to proceed out of their established networks, then too much proximity may act as a barrier (Boschma, 2005).

Figure 3.3. A hypothetical example of the Knowledge Based Urban Development (KBUD) Land Use Design Deploying the Type of Organisation as the Only Design Criteria

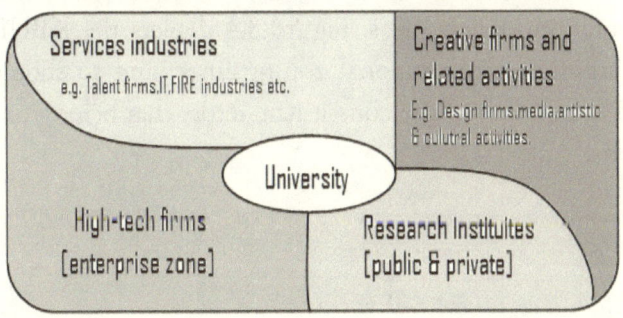

Sources: Author, 2021

Too little inter-organizational proximity raises concerns of opportunism owing to the lack of control over intellectual property and the weakening of networking capabilities among the agents that belong to similar organizations. Figure 3.3 depicts the hypothetical design of a KBUD that is divided along the lines of the organizational type of participants (Sarimin & Yigitcanlar, 2011). The closest examples of this type of urban design would be the Cooroy Lower Mill KBUD in Queensland, Australia; the La Technopole de l'Aube in France; and the Cyberjaya multimedia corridor in Selangor, Malaysia. Institutional proximity refers to the proximity that is associated at the macro level of any organizational unit. For e.g. the public research institutions, versus the private institutions, share similar values and norms (North, 1990). Such values and norms denote the comfort level within institutions that are characterized by 'a set of common habits, routines, established practices, rule or laws that regulate the relationships between individuals and groups' (Edquist & Johnson, 1997). In as much as institutional proximity can be an enabler of interactive learning among the workers concerned, then too much institutional proximity can constrain the knowledge interactions (Boschma, 2005).

A well accepted notion is that institutional environments can act as complementarities to denote the complex web of relationships among the various departments concerned. The result should pave the way for the institutional lock-in that would resist the immediate changes (Hannan & Freeman, 1977). Such inward looking hinders the development of innovation, causing institutional rigidity and leaving no room for the experimentation of new ideas. Figure 3.4 depicts the KBUD that is planned strictly on institutional zoning lines, and so should reduce the mean integration of the constituent actors that belong to different institutions.

Figure 4. A hypothetical example of the Knowledge Based Urban Development (KBUD) Land Use Design Deploying the Type of Institution as the Only Design Criteria

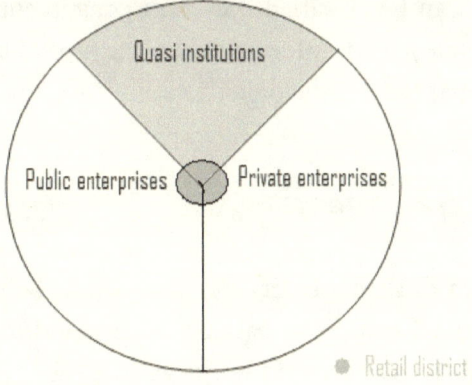

Source: Author, 2021

Geographical or spatial proximity is defined to be that physical distance between economic actors and is the most important factor, which in conjunction with other proximity factors can substantially enhance the information needs for an interactive land use design of the KBUD. Studies reiterate that short distances favors information exchange through planned or unplanned contacts and through face-to-face interactions (Audretsch & Feldman, 1996; Jaffe *et al.*, 1993; Van Oort, 2002). The temporary and permanent geographical clusterings are found to be beneficial, with the 'short distances literally bringing people together, favoring information contacts and facilitating the exchange of tacit knowledge. The larger the distance between (the) agents, the less the intensity of these positive externalities, and the more difficult it becomes to transfer tacit knowledge' (Boschma, 2005).

An urban design that creates geographical proximity between the related agents can help to initiate face-to-face interaction. Increasing distance between the related knowledge workers, caused by land use designs, can dissociate related activities in space, thereby reducing the intensity of positive externalities. Let us assume a finite system represented by a two-dimensional continuous space grid 'S'; Agents $x_1, x_2 .. x_n \in X$

X represent the number of actors that are planned in the knowledge-based development. Each agent belongs to a specific type of actor (see Table 3.1), for e.g. a technology firm or a research institution. Similarly, every agent (x_i) can be classified into their constituent properties, i.e. $i \in \{p, q, r, s\}$, where p holds information on the type of knowledge base; q, the institutional base; r, the organizational base; and s, its cognitive base. Therefore,

$$x_i = Agent_{\{p,q,r,s\}} \qquad (3.1)$$

Each agent in eq (3.1) that enters the system is to be embedded with the above and given composite parameter for identification purposes. Full information is assumed and not new. It is easily obtainable from planning documents. For e.g. and if a KBUD is being planned for 500 biomedical private firms (the private label), then 500 agents can be immediately classified to have the following characteristics:

1) analytical (knowledge base),
2) biomedical sciences (cognitive field),
3) high technology firms (organizational) and
4) private affiliation (institutional).

As agents enter the system S, they are allocated a discrete location provided by the random coordinates (x, y) To place the agents in space to maximize knowledge interactions, then the geographic proximity between agents can be represented as an inverse function of their given proximity factors, in that the more the proximity factors between any two agents (i, j) that share the same system, then the less the distance between them in space:

$$x(Agent_{ij}) \propto \frac{1}{D_{ij}} \qquad (3.2)$$

, where x represents a normalised value that is attached to each proximity factor. Eq (3.2) simply states that as the proximity factors shared between two agents (*i & j*) tends to be high, i.e. as $x \rightarrow 1$, then the (spatial) distance between agents that belong to the same institution type approaches zero, i.e. $D_{ij} \rightarrow 0$. To prevent the 'lock-in' phenomenon, as discussed previously, the extreme case should be avoided. The land use design criteria should be able to strike a balance in determining the geographical distance between agents that share similar characteristics.

Urban design that can induce greater KI levels among participating agents in the knowledge-based development should follow Figure 3.5's nonlinear curve. From interactive learning and proximity dynamics, an urban design's interaction level regarding each proximity factor would increase up to a threshold, after which it decreases steadily. The '0' on the x-axis of Figure 3.5 exhibits a design scenario that offers a minimum level of interaction, owing to the low levels of proximity among actors of the urban design. The '1' corresponds to a maximum level of proximity, showing similarly low levels of interaction. An optimal design approach would be to mix the planned KBUD participants to produce a satisfactory mix of all proximity factors, represented by the shaded region, w, in Figure 3.5.

Figure 3.5. Theoretical Urban Design Criteria for a Knowledge Interactive Environment, w

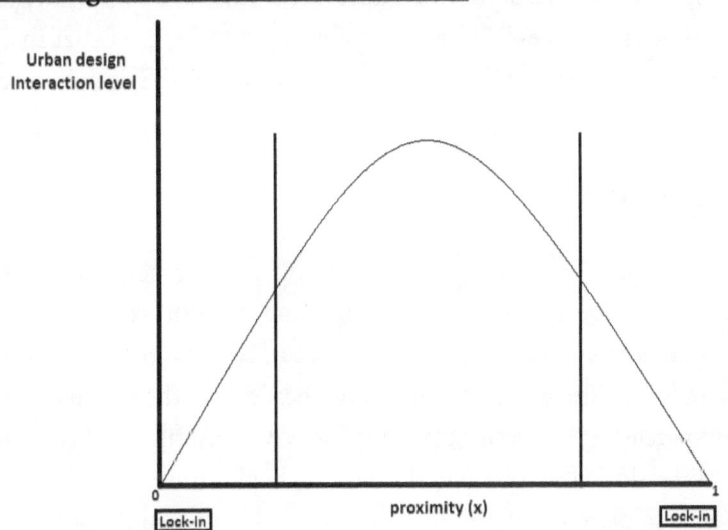

Source: Author, (2021)

The urban design outcome depends on the planner's decision as to which basis he wants to mix the land uses. For e.g. if the planner only aims for complete institutional proximity, i.e. $I(x \rightarrow 1)$ between agents in the design, then the KBUD would permit agents of the same institutions to co-locate.[5] To maximize the knowledge and information interactions, the objective is to create an urban design that positions the most related actors (i.e. actors related on more than one proximity dimension) would be close to each other. Summarizing and to attain an optimal land use design, the spatial position of all agents in the system must be governed by a minimization function (see the approach section below), which minimizes the mean linear distance between any two agents that are related by one or more levels of proximity. This way, the agents that are more closely related would be placed together, as opposed to the agents that do not share any similarity in their type of scientific or economic field, their organization or institution. Few inferences can be made from Chapter 3's foregoing considerations. A land use plan designed only on institutional lines should create physical barriers to the cross fertilization of ideas across the actors belonging to different institutions. This does not mean that such interactions would not occur but safe to say that the physical design may not be able to reinforce existing connections in space between related activities. To show the inherent complexity of the physical design process, a formal model can be proposed that includes not only the design criteria but also other facets of the design process.

The Approach

Traditionally, urban planning, design and development master plans normally include projections of population growth, the allocation of specific activities across space (i.e. the design), and that the corresponding demand for future services would altogether inform the adequate zoning of land parcels. 19th century planning ideas were useful when the growth rates were slow and predictable, but such planning ideas do pose a challenge to planners, who today encounter dynamic and unpredictable

---

5   See Figure 6.

growth rates. The situation is true for a complex industrial real estate development. The KBUD accommodates a variety of activities and it is in a constant state of change, owing to economic uncertainty. In this time and age, it would not be an exaggeration to state that long term master plans and urban designs end up on the bookshelves and closets of the direct real estate developer, because these plans and designs are hardly used as a guide to inform the future path of design and urban development (Torres, 2006). As a result, planned direct real estate developments lose their design goals because the static urban development plans are incompatible with the KBUD's dynamically changing complex system.

Cities are complex systems based on their characteristics of self-similarity, self-organization and of the emergence of patterns, which can be exhibited by the non- linear behavior of land use demand over time (Batty & Longley, 1994). KBUDs are large, self- sustaining enclaves with as many land uses as a city itself, and with some KBUDs scaling up to as big as mini cities (for e.g. Seoul's Digital Media City KBUD). There are many advantages in adopting agent-based modeling (ABM) over simple linear systems and applying the resultant models to develop planning tools that help to plan complex systems. ABM helps to gain knowledge about the dynamics of the land use design process. The modelling is often conducted in conjunction with an integrated geographic information system (GIS) (the spatial dimension) and with temporal dynamics (the time dimension) that arise from the agent–agent and agent–environment interactions (Torres, 2006). Earlier land use design models that adopt the single and multiple equation systems are found to lack the meaningful feedback mechanism, supported by dynamic ABM.

According to Schlager (1965), the land use design model (LUDM) is a 'conscious synthesis of urban form to meet human needs'. The KBUD has the need to maximize interaction via minimizing the space between related actors, who may engage in useful interactions on a frequent basis. Earlier LUDMs adopted linear programming techniques to generate optimal urban designs for a set of design goals under certain capacity constraints. E.g.s include those by Schlager (1965), Barber (1976), Arad and Berechman (1978), Williams *et al.* (2004), Makowski, *et al.* (2000), Janssen *et al.* (2008), Diamond and Wright (1988), Correia and Madden (1985), Davis and Grant (1987). Chapter 3 proposes the ABM that has inherent advantages over the simple equation-based modelling approach in addressing spatial and temporal dynamics. The ABM is a multi-agent systems model, adopted to model various social and economic problems. Well known ABM applications are found but that they are not limited to the organizational behavior field (Hughes *et al.*, 2012); to the supply chain optimization (Fox et al., 2000); to consumer behavior (Said *et al.*, 2002); to portfolio management (*Niu et al., 2003*); to pedestrian flow (Batty, 2003); to traffic congestion and management (Dresner & Stone, 2004). Only recently has Ligtenberg *et al.* (2004), demonstrate the ABM use and applicability to resolve spatial planning problems.

The land use design model (LUDM) attempts to plan for a set of well-defined n number of agents or state variables. The agents enter the system for a given period either in a continuous or in a discrete manner (groups):

$$\int_0^n Agents = x_1, x_2, x_3 \ldots \ldots x_n \qquad (3.3)$$

The basic components of a LUDM in Figure 3.6 can be denoted via deploying three sets of variables, namely, quality, quantity and location. These variables constitute the overall urban design model (Schlager, 1965). The quality variable represents the *type* of land use in demand, for e.g. the demand for industrial real estate research park space to host future biomedical research activity that may require high specification industrial land uses. Full information is assumed for the type of actors and their characteristics, as expressed in eq (3.4), Their land use demand can be determined by the number and the type of actors that enter the system, as expressed in the following manner:

$$G_i = \beta_0 x_1 + \beta_2 x_2 + \beta_3 x_3 \ldots \ldots \beta_n x_n \qquad (3.4)$$

, where G_i denotes the total land use demand for the planning region. The coefficients $x_1 \ldots n$ denote the individual demand for each type of land use (i.e. industrial high technology, residential and office space), along with the specific constant β_x that represent the subsidiary service ratio coefficients, for e.g. the streets, toilets and open space.[lx]

Figure 3.6. A System Diagram of the Agent Based Land Use Design Planning Process

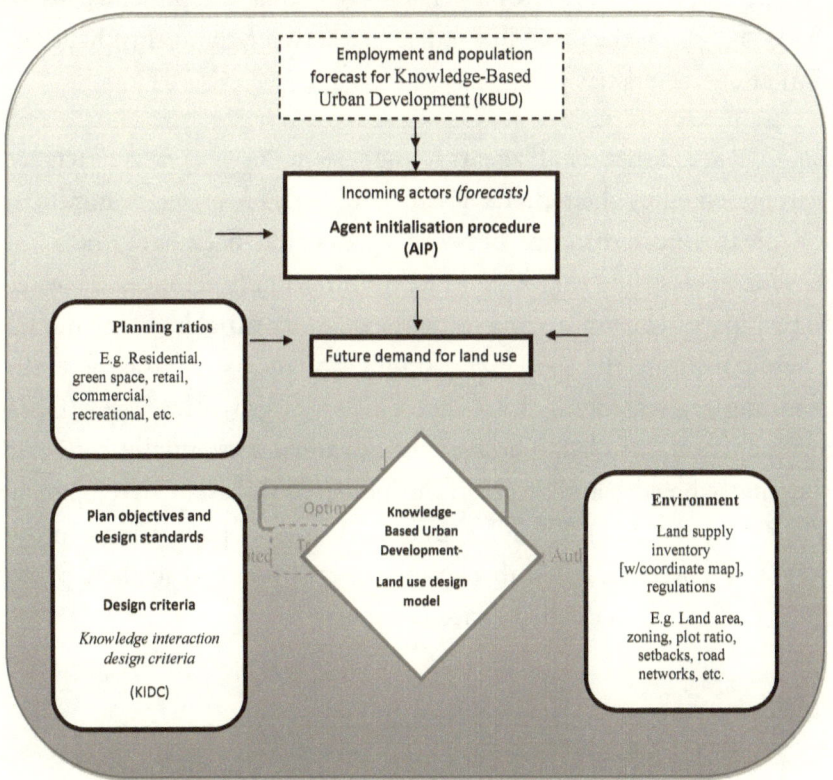

Source: Adapted and modified from Schlager (1965); Author, 2021

The land use type is derived from the set of agents entering the system G_i. The location variable is denoted by the interaction term, implying which agents are more compatible than others. Agents are enabled to share the same characteristics to co-locate in space, and from which the complementary land uses can be inferred. An optimal design criterion needs to create an equal trade-off between the four proximity factors among all agents in the system. Once the optimal system design criterion is imposed, the agents are subjected to the following minimization function in eq (3.5):

$$Min \; \overline{D}_{p,q,r,s} \sum_{i=2}^{n} (x_i) \qquad (3.5)$$

, where the term x_i denotes a generic agent that is represented by eq (3.5). $\overline{D}_{p,q,r,s}$ is the mean linear distance between the agents that share similar characteristics p, q, r, s.

Eq. (3.5) states that for all agents in the system, $x_{1,2...n} \in X$, each can be represented by their characteristic parameters p, q, r, s, to minimize the mean linear distance between agents that belong to the same parameter class (i.e. p, q, r, s). The minimization function is subjected to two spatial constraints, denoting the quantity variables of the model. These constitute the spatial constraints on land parcels or the entire planning region (for e.g. plot area, plot ratio, gross floor area (GFA) and population limits). These quantity variables essentially constrain the length, breadth and height of the industrial real estate development. They are given either through the eq (3.6) regional population controls (i.e. person per acre, F_N) or through the upper limits on each land parcel in eq (3.7), such as the plot ratios (x_i):

$$\sum_{x_0}^{n} n_x < F_N \qquad (3.6)$$

$$x_1 + x_2 + x_3 ... x_n \leq F_x \qquad (3.7)$$

, where n **is the total population expected of the proposed industrial real estate development and** F_N is the artificial limit imposed. F_x is the upper limit that restricts the buildable height on land parcels.

The alternative in planning practice can be taken to be the gross floor area (GFA) ratio and/or the plot ratio (PR). A generalized planning approach for the proposed KBUD-LUDM that adopts ABM is depicted in a system diagram of Figure 3.6. The employment and population forecasts are external to the KBUD-LUDM and are assumed to be the given inputs. They include information about the number of and the types of industries planned (i.e. the knowledge bases), the types of organizations that are expected to be accommodated (for e.g. the technology firms, the services and the RIs), the participating institutions (for e.g. the public, private and quasi institutions), along with their respective industrial classification of their scientific fields or economic sectors (i.e. the cognitive bases). Such an information set generates an approximate number of and the types of agents that are expected to participate in the KBUD - agent initialization procedure (AIP). The second set of inputs constitutes geographical information on the land parcels (i.e. the coordinate map) and their corresponding constraints (for e.g. plot ratios, height restrictions and the real estate asset conservation list.). The input set are optimized[lxi] to generate a spatial design that satisfies the urban design goal of maximizing the knowledge interaction design criteria (KIDC). It is readily observed how other constraints may be required to generate a more comprehensive KBUD design. The literature shows that the cost constraints constitute a favorable option for the land use design optimization problem. Compatible soil types and the transportation constraints can be considered (Diamond & Wright, 1988; Opdam *et al.,* **2006; Schlager, 1965;** *Williams et al., 2004).*

The Primary Data Requirement

A detailed rendition of land use design as an output is crucial in achieving widespread acceptance by urban planners and public authorities (Schlager, 1965). Chapter 3 outlines the required data (i.e. the input parameters) for the KBUD-LUDM) to generate meaningful land use designs. Three primary datasets are required to support the numerical, computational process. Such datasets include the spatial information on demarcated land parcels and its location on the planned site i.e. of the CityCAD 2.2.3 software

program, 2014 and 2020. Regional economic forecasts or essentially an approximate number of participants and their characteristics that are planned for the industrial real estate development.

Additional input data include the physical constraints, such as the supra urban density restrictions for e.g. the plot ratios, height restrictions and building setbacks; the gross floor area (GFA) and the government's reserved sites that are to be avoided i.e. land that is unsuitable for direct real estate development and the conservation sites. Minimum requirements include supplementary land uses like the number of libraries, seminar halls, cafes, retail outlets, car parks, lot coverage and green spaces. Collectively, such land uses from the local or regional planning authorities enable a more comprehensive urban design.

Concluding Comments

21st century urban planners look to the knowledge-based urban development (KBUD) as a new form of urban renewal for industrial cities, to bring about sustainable economic prosperity and socio spatial order to the contemporary city.[lxii] Inefficient large urban designs of planned post-industrial clusters have the undesirable outcome of creating the dissociation of related activities. Physical barriers can be on the rise that lead to a reduced level of intra cluster knowledge interactions via planned and spontaneous channels. Chapter 3 addresses the growing need for an urban design criterion that enables efficient land use planning for the KBUDs. Planned mixed-use land use designs can shape the knowledge interactions (KIs) between different types of actors by placing the 'related' workers together.

From the literature on the different actors, a unique urban design criterion can be developed, aimed at enhancing the knowledge interactions (KIs) of the KBUDs. Chapter 3 defines the KBUD 'actors' in terms of their specific roles in the KBUD innovation ecosystem. Drawing on the innovation and proximity dynamics literature, Chapter 3 proposes the knowledge interaction design criteria (KIDC) to enable urban planners to associate the related actors in space. With such a KIDC, the important rationale is satisfied when performing land use zoning 'to integrate compatible land uses, which generate positive externalities so that they are mutually beneficial (Chung, 1994)'.[lxiii]

Chapter 3 offers a formal representation of the knowledge based urban development-land use design model (KBUD-LUDM), incorporating the KI interaction design criteria, the KDIC via adopting agent-based modelling (ABM), to obtain the optimal land use design solutions. The contribution to urban planning and the KBUD design is twofold. First, Chapter 3 discusses how to identify and classify the complementary actors (i.e. the group) in a planned post-industrial KBUD. Secondly, Chapter 3 offers a dynamic alternative planning approach to 'zone' the KBUD via adopting the agent-based model, ABM (Barber, 1976; Diamond & Wright, 1988; Janssen *et al.*, **2008).**

(The author wishes to acknowledge his appreciation to Dr Rengarajan Satyanarain, *a former NUS research scholar, and presently a management information system consultant; for his meaningful contribution and perseverance in sourcing* the related literature, *the required primary data and for the initial analysis).*

References

Abukhater, A. B. E.-D. (2009). Rethinking planning theory and practice: a glimmer of light for Prospects of integrated planning to combat complex urban realities. *Theoretical and Empirical Researches in Urban Management, 4*(2 (11)), 64-79.

Allen, T. J. (1984). Managing the flow of technology: Technology transfer and the dissemination of technological information within the R&D organization. *MIT Press Books, 1.*

Ancona, D. G., & Caldwell, D. F. (1992). Bridging the boundary: External activity and performance in organizational teams. *Administrative science quarterly*, 634-665.

Anselin, L., Varga, A., & Acs, Z. (1997). Local geographic spillovers between university research and high technology innovations. *Journal of Urban Economics, 42*(3), 422-448.

Asheim, & Gertler, M. (2005). The geography of innovation. *The Oxford handbook of innovation*, 291-317.

Asheim, B., Coenen, L., & Vang, J. (2007). Face-to-face, buzz, and knowledge bases: sociospatial implications for learning, innovation, and innovation policy. *Environment and Planning C, 25*(5), 655.

Bajracharya, B., & Too, L. I., J. . (2009). Developing Knowledge Precincts in Regional Towns: Opportunities and Challenges. *paper presented at the 2ⁿᵈ International Urban Design*.

Barber, G. (1976). Land-use plan design via interactive multiple-objective programming. *Environment and Planning A, 8*(6), 625-636.

Bathelt, H., Malmberg, A., & Maskell, P. (2004). Clusters and knowledge: local buzz, global pipelines and the process of knowledge creation. *Progress in Human geography, 28*(1), 31-56.

Batty, M. (2003). Agent-based pedestrian modelling. *Advanced spatial analysis: The CASA book of GIS*, 81-106.

Boschma, R. (2005). Proximity and innovation: a critical assessment. *Regional studies, 39*(1), 61-74.

Bottazzi, L., & Peri, G. (2003). Innovation and spillovers in regions: Evidence from European patent data. *European Economic Review, 47*(4), 687-710.

Cantwell, J., & Santangelo, G. D. (2003). The new geography of corporate research in information and communications technology (ICT) *Change, Transformation and Development* (pp. 343-377): Springer.

Carrillo, F. J. (2004). Capital cities: a taxonomy of capital accounts for knowledge cities. *Journal of Knowledge Management, 8*(5), 28-46.

Chatzkel, J. (2004). Greater Phoenix as a knowledge capital. *Journal of Knowledge Management, 8*(5), 61-72.

Cheng, P., Choi, C. J., Chen, S., Eldomiaty, T. I., & Millar, C. C. (2004). Knowledge repositories in knowledge cities: institutions, conventions and knowledge subnetworks. *Journal of Knowledge Management, 8*(5), 96-106.

Cohen, W. M., & Levinthal, D. A. (1990). Absorptive capacity: a new perspective on learning and innovation. *Administrative science quarterly*, 128-152.

Cooke, P. (2001). Regional innovation systems, clusters, and the knowledge economy. *Industrial and corporate change, 10*(4), 945-974.

Cooke, P., Uranga, M. G., & Etxebarria, G. (1998). Regional systems of innovation: an evolutionary perspective. *Environment and Planning A, 30*, 1563-1584.

Correia, P., & Madden, M. (1985). Optimisation of land purchasing and management using mixed integer programming: a case study in a Portuguese municipal authority. *Environment and Planning B: Planning and Design, 12*(3), 335-349.

den Hertog, P. (2002). 10. Co-producers of innovation: on the role of knowledge-intensive business services in innovation. *Productivity, innovation and knowledge in services: New economic and socio-economic approaches,* 223.

Dresner, K., & Stone, P. (2004). *Multiagent traffic management: A reservation-based intersection control mechanism.* Paper presented at the Proceedings of the Third International Joint Conference on Autonomous Agents and Multiagent Systems-Volume 2.

Duffy, F., Jaunzens, D., Laing, A., & Willis, S. (2012). *New environments for working*: Taylor & Francis.

Elfring, T., & Hulsink, W. (2003). Networks in entrepreneurship: the case of high-technology firms. *Small business economics, 21*(4), 409-422.

Etzkowitz, H., & Leydesdorff, L. (2000). The dynamics of innovation: from National Systems and "Mode 2" to a Triple Helix of university–industry–government relations. *Research Policy, 29*(2), 109-123.

Foray, D. (2005). Economic fundamentals of the knowledge society. *Informationsgesellschaft. Geschichten und Wirklichkeit. Fribourg. S,* 211-240.

Fox, M. S., Barbuceanu, M., & Teigen, R. (2000). Agent-oriented supply-chain management. *International Journal of Flexible Manufacturing Systems, 12*(2-3), 165-188.

Garcia, B. C. (2004). Developing futures: a knowledge-based capital for Manchester. *Journal of Knowledge Management, 8*(5), 47-60.

Hertog, P. d. (2000). Knowledge-intensive business services as co-producers of innovation. *International Journal of Innovation Management, 4*(04), 491-528.

Hillier, B., O'Sullivan, P., Penn, A., Kolokotroni, M., Rasmussen, M., & Xu, J. (1990). The design of research laboratories.

Hughes, H. P., Clegg, C. W., Robinson, M. A., & Crowder, R. M. (2012). Agent-based modelling and simulation: The potential contribution to organizational psychology. *Journal of Occupational and Organizational Psychology, 85*(3), 487-502.

Isaksen, A. (2004). Knowledge-based clusters and urban location: the clustering of software consultancy in Oslo. *Urban Studies, 41*(5-6), 1157-1174.

Janssen, R., van Herwijnen, M., Stewart, T. J., & Aerts, J. (2008). Multiobjective decision support for land-use planning. *ENVIRONMENT AND PLANNING B PLANNING AND DESIGN, 35*(4), 740.

Kesidou, E., Caniëls, M. C., & Romijn, H. A. (2009). Local Knowledge Spillovers and Development: An Exploration of the Software Cluster in Uruguay: Research Paper. *Industry and Innovation, 16*(2), 247-272.

Knight, R. V. (1995). Knowledge-based development: policy and planning implications for cities. *Urban Studies, 32*(2), 225-260.

Lawson, C., & Lorenz, E. (1999). Collective learning, tacit knowledge and regional innovative capacity. *Regional studies, 33*(4), 305-317.

Levitt, B., & March, J. G. (1988). Organizational learning. *Annual review of sociology,* 319-340.

Ligtenberg, A., Wachowicz, M., Bregt, A. K., Beulens, A., & Kettenis, D. L. (2004). A design and application of a multi-agent system for simulation of multi-actor spatial planning. *Journal of Environmental Management, 72*(1), 43-55.

Makowski, D., Hendrix, E. M., van Ittersum, M. K., & Rossing, W. A. (2000). A framework to study nearly optimal solutions of linear programming models developed for agricultural land use exploration. *Ecological Modelling, 131*(1), 65-77.

Malmberg, A., & Maskell, P. (2006). Localized learning revisited. *Growth and Change, 37*(1), 1-18.

Mascitelli, R. (2000). From experience: harnessing tacit knowledge to achieve breakthrough innovation. *Journal of product innovation management, 17*(3), 179-193.

Meeus, M., Oerlemans, L., & Hage, J. (2004). Industry-public knowledge infrastructure interaction: intra-and inter-organizational explanations of interactive learning. *Industry and Innovation, 11*(4), 327-352.

Moodysson, J., Coenen, L., & Asheim, B. (2008). Explaining spatial patterns of innovation: analytical and synthetic modes of knowledge creation in the Medicon Valley life-science cluster. *Environment and Planning A, 40*(5), 1040-1056.

Muller, E., & Zenker, A. (2001a). Business services as actors of knowledge transformation: the role of KIBS in regional and national innovation systems. *Research Policy, 30*(9), 1501-1516.

Muller, E., & Zenker, A. (2001b). Business services as actors of knowledge transformation: the role of KIBS in regional and national innovation systems. *Research Policy, 30*(9), 2.

Niu, X., McCalla, G., & Vassileva, J. (2003). Purpose-based user modelling in a multi-agent portfolio management system *User Modeling 2003* (pp. 398-402): Springer.

Oerlemans, L. A., Meeus, M. T., & Boekema, F. W. (2001). Firm clustering and innovation: Determinants and effects*. *Papers in regional science, 80*(3), 337-356.

Opdam, P., Steingröver, E., & Rooij, S. v. (2006). Ecological networks: a spatial concept for multi-actor planning of sustainable landscapes. *Landscape and urban planning, 75*(3), 322-332.

Rashid, M., Kampschroer, K., & Zimring, C. (2006). Spatial layout and face-to-face interaction in offices-a study of the mechanisms of spatial effects on face-to-face interaction. *ENVIRONMENT AND PLANNING B PLANNING AND DESIGN, 33*(6), 825.

Rees, J., & Stafford, H. A. (1986). Location: their relevance for understanding high-technology complexes. *Technology, regions, and policy*, 23.

Said, L. B., Bouron, T., & Drogoul, A. (2002). *Agent-based interaction analysis of consumer behavior.* Paper presented at the Proceedings of the first international joint conference on Autonomous agents and multiagent systems: part 1.

Salter, A., & Gann, D. (2003). Sources of ideas for innovation in engineering design. *Research Policy, 32*(8), 1309-1324.

Sarimin, M., & Yigitcanlar, T. (2011). Knowledge-based urban development of Multimedia Super Corridor, Malaysia: an overview. *International Journal of Knowledge-Based Development, 2*(1), 34-48.

Searle, G., & Pritchard, B. (2008). Beyond planning: Sydney's knowledge sector development.

Segal, N. S., Smilor, R., Kozmetsky, G., & Gibson, D. (1988). The Cambridge Phenomenon: universities, research, and local economic development in Great Britain. *Creating the Technopolis. Ballinger, Cambridge (Massachusetts)*, 81-90.

Shaw, A. T., & Gilly, J.-P. (2000). On the analytical dimension of proximity dynamics. *Regional studies, 34*(2), 169-180.

Simon, H. A. (1955). A behavioral model of rational choice. *the Quarterly journal of Economics, 69*(1), 99-118.

Torre, A., & Rallet, A. (2005). Proximity and localization. *Regional studies, 39*(1), 47-59.

Wigand, R. T. (1988). High technology development in the Phoenix area: Taming the desert. *Creating the Technopolis. Ballinger, Cambridge (Massachusetts)*, 185-202.

Williams, J. C., ReVelle, C. S., & Levin, S. A. (2004). Using mathematical optimization models to design nature reserves. *Frontiers in Ecology and the Environment, 2*(2), 98-105.

Yigitcanlar, T. (2009). Planning for knowledge-based urban development: global perspectives. *Journal of Knowledge Management, 13*(5), 228-242.

Chapter 4

The Knowledge-Based Urban Development-Land Use Design Model (KBUD-LUDM) – Singapore's Biopolis At The One North Knowledge-Based Development (KBUD)

Chapter 4 highlights several essential contributions to the design and planning literature of post-industrial clusters. The Chapter also discusses the simulation results and findings of the 'Knowledge-Based Urban Development-Land Use Design Model' (KBUD-LUDM) utilizing Singapore's 'One North' knowledge-based urban development (KBUD). Chapter 4 is presented in five parts and with the first part discussing the basic assumptions of the KBUD-LUDM that are required to initialize and conduct scenario analysis. The second part deals with the baseline scenario simulation-step of the One North KBUD. Such a model's agent initialization procedure (AIP) is estimated from surveys and interviews.

The third part constructs the baseline scenario, which is used as a benchmark to project scenarios of plausible future states of the One

North KBUD. This third part demonstrates the KBUD-LUDM's flexibility in performing incremental planning as land-use demand fluctuates over time. The fourth part looks into the validation and visualization procedures of future states of the One North KBUD, adopting the KBUD-LUDM. The fifth part concludes Chapter 4 by summarizing the study, the questions, the approach, the results and findings. Several directions for extending the KBUD-LUDM via the inclusion of multiple design criteria, for the comprehensive multi-dimensional land-use design modelling, are discussed.

The Model Assumptions

Planning models that attempt to simulate future scenarios for Knowledge-Based Urban Developments (KBUDs), require some basic assumptions about the incoming actors. These help planners estimate the necessary space, the type of land uses to be accommodated, the amenities and other infrastructural requirements. Key assumptions of the knowledge-based urban development-land use design model (KBUD-LUDM) are offered in conjunction with agent-based modeling.

It is imperative that such a model discusses the general classification of the agents, which participate in the KBUD. The minimum space requirements of both types of agents, namely the primary and secondary agents, are also discussed via adopting simple planning ratio techniques.

The Agent characteristics
All actors in the KBUD comprise the primary and secondary agents. The primary agents can be further divided into four major types based on their organizational nature like the:

(i)   technology firm,
(ii)   research institution,
(iii)   educational institution and
(iv)   the service firm.

Therefore, each primary agent entering the KBUD-LUDM has a unique set of characteristics that provides the heterogeneity required to represent all types of actors of the knowledge-based urban development (KBUD). Figure 4.1 is a modified version representing the agent characteristics deployed in the One North knowledge-based urban development-land use design model (KBUD-LUDM). As information on the different types of the cognitive base is unavailable, it is reasonable to leave them out of the model for simplification purposes. Similarly, the institutional differentiation is limited to the public and private institutions instead of the private, public and quasi institutions. This is because going through the masterplans, no evidence can be found of the One North KBUD to even hosting the quasi i.e. private-public institutional actors. To summarize, the agent characteristics specified in the KBUD-LUDM) are provided in Figure 4.1, which depicts a hypothetical declared, *agent$_i$*, containing information about the knowledge base, the institutional base and organizational base, because the agents enter the KBUD-LUDM via the agent initialization procedure (AIP).

Space Requirements for Primary and Secondary Agents
The agent-based KBUD-LUDM for the One North KBUD is modeled on several essential assumptions, which are required for a holistic design approach. Such assumptions are standard urban planning ratios, related to space requirements that remain constant through every cycle of simulation. All agents in the system can be classified into primary agents and secondary (subsidiary) agents. The primary agents include the technology firm (for e.g. the bio engineering and information technology, IT, firms); the research institution (for e.g. the basic and applied research firms); the educational institution (for e.g. schools, universities and polytechnics); and the service firm (for e.g. the finance, insurance and real estate, FIRE, industry firms; the talent firms and the networking services firms. Table 4.2 depicts the space requirements for the primary agents according to their organization type deployed in the knowledge-based urban development-land use design model (KBUD-LUDM).

Figure 4.1 Defining the actor/agent characteristics in the Knowledge-Based Urban Development-Land Use Design Model (KBUD-LUDM) agent-based modl

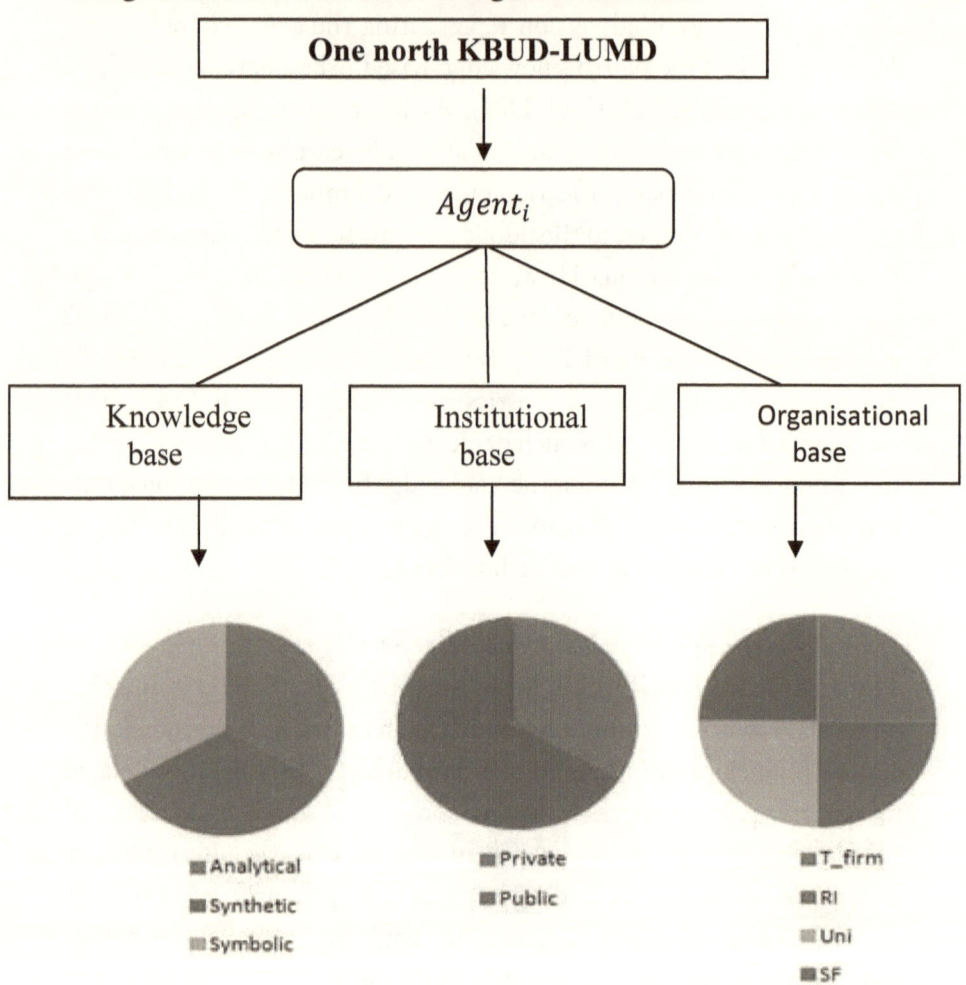

Source: Author, 2021

Table 4.2. The Primary Agent Classification and Planning Parameters Assumption Table

Primary Agent Type	Assumptions
Technology firm	• Minimum unit of occupation: firm • Minimum number of persons/firm: 15 • Space per person: 120 sq ft • Minimum space per agent = 1,500 sq ft
Research institution	• Unit of occupation: department/NGO • Minimum number of persons/departments: 10 • Space per person: 120 sq ft • Minimum space per agent = 1,200 sq ft
Educational institution (School, university etc.)	• Unit of occupation: department • Minimum number of persons/department: 10 • Space per person: 100 sq ft • Minimum space per agent = 1,200 sq ft
Miscellaneous service industries (legal, venture capitalists, talent agencies, FIRE[6], etc.)	• Unit of occupation: firm • Minimum number of persons/firms: 13 • Space per person: 100 sq ft • Minimum space per agent = 1,300 sq ft

The first required parameter for each type of primary agent is the minimum unit of occupation stating what type of tenant entity it belongs to i.e. what is the type of the occupying primary agent like a firm or department. The second parameter is the *minimum number of persons* required for each primary agent type to enable urban planners to get an idea of the space needed for the incoming actors. The *space per person* parameter is a constant, usually assumed in master plans for different types of activity.

---

6   The abbreviation FIRE stands for finance, insurance and real estate services.

The knowledge-based urban development-land use design model (KBUD-LUDM) requires minimum standards to estimate the total buildable space for each land unit. While it is true that these minimum standards may not be optimal for other cities, such minimum standards are affirmed for the One North KBUD in Singapore. The standards themselves are sourced from primary and extensive consultations with the Jurong Town Corporation (JTC) planners. The Space per agent (SPA) associated with every agent represents the total amount of minimum space required (in sq ft) for each primary agent, entering the knowledge-based urban development (KBUD) system in eq (4.1):

$$
\begin{aligned}
&\textit{Space per agent (SPA)} = \\
&\textit{Minimum number of persons per unit} \times \\
&\textit{Space per person}
\end{aligned}
\tag{4.1}
$$

The subsidiary agents represent the supporting land uses like the retail/commercial, recreational services and green space requirements. From urban planning and in general, the number of subsidiary land-uses always depends on the extent of the space used for primary purposes. Some e.g.s would be the minimum space per worker, the minimum bathrooms per 1,000 people, and the minimum space for retail/commercial space per 1,000 people. It is common practice to use standard planning ratios to maintain minimum standards throughout the masterplan. Such standard planning ratios are often derived after considering many aspects of a knowledge-based urban development (KBUD), like the space availability, urban density, activity mapping and age cohort studies. For the case of Singapore's One North KBUD, the standard planning ratios are duly estimated from the Jurong Town Corporation (JTC) detailed land-use plans, which would have already taken the cost aspects into consideration, prior to generating the zoning maps (JTC, 2010 and 2021).

According to the JTC, the expected population at then On North KBUD ranges from a hundred thousand to two hundred thousand people i.e. residents and workers by the end of nearly thirty years (2003–2030). JTC's detailed land-use plan allocates gross floor ratios (GFAs) for parks, retail, sports and recreation in Table 4.2. Assuming the minimum one hundred-thousand value, and if one simply divides the total allocated space of secondary land uses by the expected population, one obtains the minimum space required for the park/retail/recreation and sports per person for the 200-hectare One North KBUD site. Such a minimum space required can be utilized as a constant planning ratio to service the population of the primary agents.

Therefore, the secondary agents i.e. subsidiary land uses in the knowledge-based urban development-land use design model (KBUD-LUDM) is initialized as shown in the ratios of Table 4.2. The Table can be understood with an e.g. in that if there are 10 technology firms located in a land unit, then with respect to Table 4.2, each technology-firm agent can on average consists of 15 people.

Table 4.2. Assumptions For Secondary Agents in The Agent Initialization Procedure (AIP)

Variable name	Residents	Green space/ Parks	Retail	Sports and recreation
Expected population @ One north[1]	100,000			
GFA – Total planned development (sq m)[2]		1,35,466	1,10,023	1,09,302
Space per person (sq m)		1.35	1.1	1.09
Approximated GFA		1,35,000	1,10,000	1,09,000
Percentage deviation				
Secondary agents planning ratio (minimum space required per person)		Agent 2 sq m	Agent 1.1 sq m	Agent 1.09 sq m

Source: JTC (2010) and Author, 2021.

The total space demand of the secondary agents for the following land uses is estimated in eqs (4.2) to (4.4):

$$Parks = 300 \; sq \; m \; (10{\times}15{\times}2 \; sq \; m) \qquad (4.2)$$

$$Retail = 165 \; sq \; m \; (10{\times}15{\times}1.1 \; sq \; m) \qquad (4.3)$$

$$Sports \; and \; recreation = 163.5 \; sq \; m \; (10{\times}15{\times}1.09 \; sq \; m) \qquad (4.4)$$

In the agent-based model, a secondary agent is created for every primary agent, with an intrinsic value of the minimum space requirement. The same for the case of the parks/green space, in which 15 agents each with 2 sq m of space requirement is initialized. Housing needs are essential to sustain a 24-hour vibrancy in any knowledge-based urban development (KBUD). Empirical studies have found that the knowledge-based workers on average tend to locate much closer to their workplaces, attributable to the non-routine type of work patterns associated with their jobs. Post-industrial districts are gearing towards live-work-play designs to be compatible with the workers' non-routine nature by offering amenities and housing, closer to work. The master plan of Singapore's One North KBUD seeks to house 30% of its workers within the 200-hectare KBUD site to enable work–life balance. It is essential to note that Singapore is one hundred percent urbanized, and that the One North KBUD site is surrounded by public and private estates that service the One North KBUD workers on-site.

Table 4.3 shows the different types of housing that are planned to accommodate the One North KBUD workforce. The housing types include the apartments or condominium units, the detached housing and semi-detached landed housing. As land is scarce and is expensive in Singapore, the condominiums/apartments should satisfy most of the housing needs at the One North KBUD workforce at around twenty percent of the resident population. Semi-detached and detached housing, deemed for the dual live–work purpose, would service a mere ten percent of the total resident housing population of the One North KBUD.

Table 4.3. The Assumptions for The Secondary Agents (Housing Only) In The Agent Initialization Procedure (AIP)

Agent	Type of housing	Percentage of residents serviced (%)	Number of people serviced	Space per person (sq ft)	Total space per agent (sq ft)
Housing	Apartment/ condominium	20	3	350	1,200
	Detached housing	5	4	500	2,000
	Semi-detached housing	5	6	300	1,800

Source: Author, 2021

A simple e,g. is to assume that 15 technology firms are planned on-site at the One North KBUD. As there are 150 workers in total, the number of apartment units that needs to service the workers would be 30, resulting in a total GFA of 31,500 square feet. Similar calculations bring the space required for the detached and semi-detached housing to 15,000 and 13,500 square feet respectively:

$$\text{Apartment/condominium} = 36,000 \; GFA$$
$$((10 \times (15 \times 0.20))) \times 1,200 \qquad (4.5)$$

$$\text{Detached housing} = 15,000 \; GFA \; ((10 \times (15 \times 0.05))) \times 2,000 \qquad (4.6)$$

$$\text{Semi-detached housing} = 13,500 \; GFA$$
$$((10 \times (15 \times 0.05))) \times 1,800 \qquad (4.7)$$

The discussion has so far looked at several planning ratios that would be used to initialize the baseline model of the One North KBUD. As the knowledge-based urban development-land use design model (KBUD-LUDM) is a planning model, which attempts to simulate future planned scenarios, the assumptions stipulated herewith are necessary as a starting point to demonstrate the model's capacity, to generate optimal design solutions, using the knowledge interaction design criteria (KIDC) and the land-use cost criteria (LUCC). It is meaningful to bear in mind that the planning ratios, as the secondary agents, need not be static but can be changed to suit their potential and unique urban developmental requirements.

The Scenario Planning

Traditional master planning for urban development often relies on the belief that the application of professional expertise to achieve well-defined urban design goals, would ensure sustenance of the physical structure of the plan over time. However, urban planners often face changing local conditions and uncertain economic climates, compelling the planners to handle extraordinary surprises, which detract the urban development from its intended goals (Scott, 1998). Urban planners of Singapore's One North knowledge-based urban development (KBUD) face problematic years following the conceptual phase. The problem lies with the One North KBUD associated costs, and with the absence of demand for one or more of the land uses stipulated in One North's KBUD masterplan. Old land-use masterplans and maps must be discarded, while new land-use designs had to be redrawn to suit prevailing economic conditions, and that in the process the master planning tends to repeat itself over time. Such a master planning process often seems to be unplanned or as one planner recounted the process to be *on the fly*, leaving much room for the original land-use design to deviate from the intended planning goals.

Planning for the future can have different variations, according to the risk of the project that is undertaken by the urban planner. Peterson *et al.* (2003) classify such project risk to be four interacting phases, depending on the uncertainity and controllability during the planning process. Large scale post-industrial cluster developments tend to be riddled with high uncertainty and low controllability, owing to changes in demand, influenced by local and global economic forces. Scenario planning can therefore be adopted to consider a variety of possible outcomes, which equip the urban planner with alternative scenarios, to deal with uncertainty and enabling the urban planner to develop more resilient conservation policies but retaining the original design goals. Such alternative scenarios so enable urban planners to make decisions under uncontrollable and irreducible uncertainties.

Figure 4.5 Illustration Of Scenario Planning For The Proposed One North KBUD-LUDM

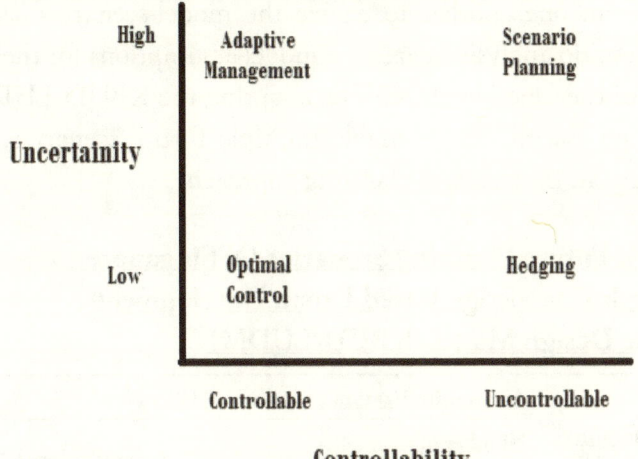

Source: Adopted from Peterson *et al.* (2003); Author (2021)

It is important to reiterate that the knowledge-based urban development-land use design model (KBUD-LUDM) of Figure 4.5, being unlike many land-use models, is not a predictive model but merely a projection model. In a prediction model, future events are predicted via adopting some basic understanding of the prevailing drivers and reasonable parameter assumptions about those drivers, given their probability distributions (Clark *et al.*, 2001).

Scenario planning for the KBUD-LUDM in practice can be conducted with a small group of research scientists, managers, policy makers and other essential stakeholders via an iterative process (Peterson *et al.*, 2003).

For the scenario analysis, an incremental storyline approach is adopted in line with the intentions of the official master plan. Projections for the future of the One North KBUD is provided in Table 4.4 in accordance with the storyline, adopted in the master plan. The complete scenario analysis using the proposed KBUD-LUDM is conducted in the subsequent sections.

The One North KBUD Case

To account for different viewpoints, a set of simulations is conducted to enable the scenario analysis. Future scenarios should be sufficiently distinct from one another to enable the model-scenarios' flexibility. Such a scenario analysis freezes the model assumptions for the baseline scenario of the One North KBUD, adopting the KBUD-LUDM, and to build on the model to enable multiple future scenarios, thereby conducting an incremental planning approach.

Table 4.4. Future Planning Scenarios Of Singapore One North Knowledge-Based Urban Development- Land Use Design Model (KBUD-LUDM)

Time horizon (in years)	Planning scenario	Agent initialization procedure [AIP]			
		Number of agents per scenario	Agent Kb Ratio	Organizational type	Public-private ratio
2003-2009	Optimistic (baseline)	2,000	$\alpha=0.5, \beta=0.5, \gamma=0$	$TF=0.30, RI=0.50, EI=0.10, SF=0.10$	80:20
2012	Pessimistic	600	$\alpha=0.40, \beta=0.40, \gamma=0.20$	$TF=0.25, RI=0.45, EI=0.20, SF=0.10$	70:30
2015	Pessimistic	1,000	$\alpha=0.30, \beta=0.30, \gamma=0.40$	$TF=0.20, RI=0.30, EI=0.15, SF=0.35$	60:40
2018	Neutral	1,600	$\alpha=0.25, \beta=0.25, \gamma=0.50$	$TF=0.40, RI=0.10, EI=0.10, SF=0.40$	50:50
2021	Optimistic	2,500	$\alpha=0.15, \beta=0.25, \gamma=0.60$	$TF=0.30, RI=0.30, EI=0.30, SF=0.10$	40:60
2024	Optimistic	3,500	$\alpha=0.25, \beta=0.25, \gamma=0.50$	$TF=0.40, RI=0.15, EI=0.15, SF=0.30$	30:70

NB. The baseline scenario is informed from past estimations of the number of actors accommodated at the One North KBUD between 2003 and 2009 through to 2024. Source; Author, 2021.

The Baseline Scenario

The baseline scenario is conducted as the benchmark for the knowledge-based urban development-land use design model (KBUD-LUDM). As shown in Table 4.4 and from the year 2012, all three phases of the Biopolis and the Fusionopolis are completed.

In the baseline scenario, model simulations are conducted for phases 1 and 2, wherein the total number of workers are estimated to be around 23,600, which demand a total workspace of 254,555 square meters for both the Biopolis and Fusionopolis combined. Ideally, the information about how many institutions, technology firms, service firms and the university departments, along with their field(s) of interest and the space that they occupy, would be meaningful to inform the agent initialization procedure (AIP). Such a primary information set is close to the survey data, collected via consultations with the senior planners of the One North KBUD planning team (see Table 4.5).

Table 4.5. Space Allocation of Phase 1 Development of The 'One North' Knowledge-Based Urban Development (KBUD)

Cluster name	Space provided	Number of workers (approximately)	Year of completion
Biopolis			
Phase 1	185,000 m²	4,500	2009
Phase 2	37,000 m²	1,000	2012
Phase 3	41,505 m²	1,000	2015
Fusionopolis			
Phase 1	120,000 m²	6,000	2010
Phase 2B	103,635 m²	5,000	2013
Phase 2A	50,000 m²	5,000	2010
Total		22,500	

Source: JTC official website & Author's survey, 2013 and 2021

For the baseline scenario, however, I was able to make reasonable assumptions after obtaining expert opinion from senior planners at the Jurong Town Corporation (JTC). The minimum planning standards that would help the knowledge-based urban development-land use design model (KBUD-LUDM) to approximate the land-use demand from incoming agents are provided in Table 4.6.

The first column of Table 4.6 shows the primary agent classification and the minimum unit of representation by their respective types. This is followed by the second, third and fourth columns respectively on the number of workers, the minimum space and the number of agents planned on site for the baseline scenario.

Figure 4.6 depicts a pie-chart of the split-up of the primary agents by their organizational type at the One North KBUD for the baseline scenario. After several interviews with the JTC senior planners of the One North KBUD planning team, an approximate pie distribution is settled for the One North's biomedical engineering and sciences sectors until year 2013 and thereafter. Attempts are made to empirically validate the approximations of Figure 4.6 and Table 4.6 by comparing them with the tenant statistics of the One North KBUD till 2013 and thereafter to 2021. Unfortunately, and owing to confidentiality reasons, the detailed tenant data of the One North KBUD is not available.

Table 4.6. The Baseline Scenario Agent Initialization Procedure (AIP) Assumptions[7]

Agent Type [MUR[8]]	Number Of Workers	Minimum Space Required Per Person (Sq Ft)	Number Of Agents	Total Space Required (Sq M)	Estimated Number Of Workers
Technology firm [firm]	15	120	600	100,335	9,000
Research institution [department]	10	120	1,000	111,484	10,000
Educational [department] (e.g. university, school, etc.)	10	100	200	18,581	2,000
Services [firm]	13	100	200	24,155	2,600
Total	NA	NA	1,000	254,555[9]	**23,600**

Source: Author's survey, 2013 and 2021

---

7   Planning ratios in Table 4.6 were obtained through expert opinion from the head of the One North KBUD planning team.
    Such planning ratios follow from local industrial planning practices.
8   MUR- Minimum unit of representation
9   This figure shows the demand for space only from primary agents.

Figure 4.6 Distribution Assumptions of Primary Agents In the 'One North' KBUD For Its Knowledge-Based Urban Development-Land Use Design Model (KBUD-LUDM), Baseline Scenario

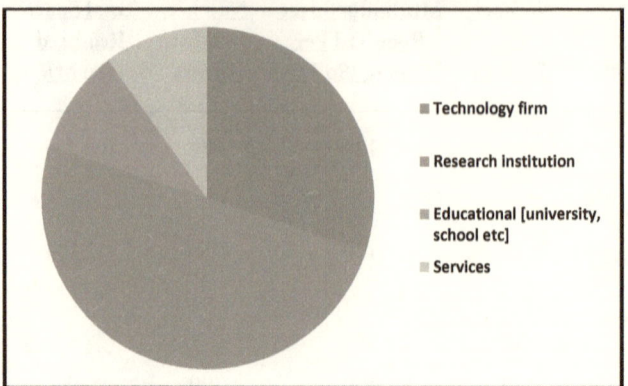

Source: Author, 2021

From the survey data, simple assumptions can made with respect to knowledge-based distribution for the One North KBUD. For e.g. Phase 1 can assume that 50% of the agents have an analytical knowledge base, and that the other 50% have a synthetic knowledge base in the One North KBUD's media and arts complex (the Mediapolis), representing the symbolic knowledge base that is nearly fully completed. The justification is the fact that the Biopolis biomedical cluster is involved in the more basic and industrial research activities, while the Fusionopolis is an applied physical sciences and engineering cluster[lxiv] . Such two clusters are the only developments at the One North KBUD till 2013. It is duly assumed that eighty percent of the agents belonging to the public sector (i.e. the public institution), is reasonable because the Singapore government, via the JTC houses most of the research institutions at the One North KBUD's Phase 1 and 2, to serve as that crucial anchor for future private investments.

The One North Baseline Simulation Results & Findings

The knowledge-based urban development-land use design model (KBUD-LUDM) specifications and outputs of the baseline scenario are provided in Table 4.7. As we can see, the model reached a solution in the first round of the land-use design optimization procedure using the earlier proposed knowledge interaction design criteria (KIDC).

The first column in Table 4.7 indicates the number of simulations (trials) it took to reach an optimal solution. The second column shows the percentage of actors with respect to their knowledge base, that is, what is the distribution of the knowledge base for the incoming agents into the Knowledge-Based Urban Development (KBUD).

Up till the first decade of development at One north, only phase 1 and 2 of Biopolis and Fusionopolis was built. As previously mentioned, 'The Biopolis' is envisioned as a core biomedical research facility conducting basic and applied scientific research that falls under the realm of the analytical base. Similarly, Fusionopolis, as described in Jurong Town Corporation (JTC)'s official website, is envisioned to be Singapore's research and development (R&D) hub for the info communication technology, media, physical sciences and engineering sectors. Therefore, a reasonable inference should be that the Fusionopolis houses mostly the synthetic type of actors.

The third knowledge-based cluster hosting symbolic agents would be the Mediapolis. As the first building of the Mediapolis started construction only by February of 2011[lxv], we will include symbolic agents for scenario analysis of future development at One north in the next section. In column two in Table 4.7, agents are split equally between the analytical and synthetic knowledge bases ($\alpha=0.5$, $\beta=0.5$), leaving the symbolic agents out of the baseline scenario ($\gamma=0$). The key empirical output variables ∂_G and σ_G in their final stages are 0.56 and 0.25 respectively.

There were around 2,044 number of simulation trials generated for the baseline KBUD-LUDM model before reaching an optimal solution. The gradual improvement of the Global delta value towards the optimum and reduction of standard deviation to the minima is graphed in Figure 4.7.

Table 4.7. Land-Use Optimization Results for The Baseline Scenario Using The Knowledge-Based Urban Development-Land Use Design Model (KBUD-LUDM)

Simulation Trials	Kb Ratio	Agents	Global Delta (∂_G)	Target ∂ $\partial_G \sim 0.50$	Std. Deviation σ_G	Optimal Design Solution
1	$\alpha=0.5$, $\beta=0.5$, $\gamma=0$	2,000	$\partial_{KB}=0.63$, $\partial_{org}=0.61$ $\partial_{inst}=0.39$	$\partial_G=0.21$	0.22	N
.		.	.	.	.	.
			.	.	.	.
2,044	$\alpha=0.5$, $\beta=0.5$, $\gamma=0$	2,000	$\partial_{KB}=0.63$, $\partial_{org}=0.61$ $\partial_{inst}=0.39$	$\partial_G=0.56$	0.25	Y

Source: Author, 2021

Figure 4.7. Graph Illustrating Total Iterations Performed Adopting The KBUD-LUDM For The Baseline Scenario Of The One North KBUD, Achieving Optimal Land Use Design ($\partial_G \sim 0.50$)

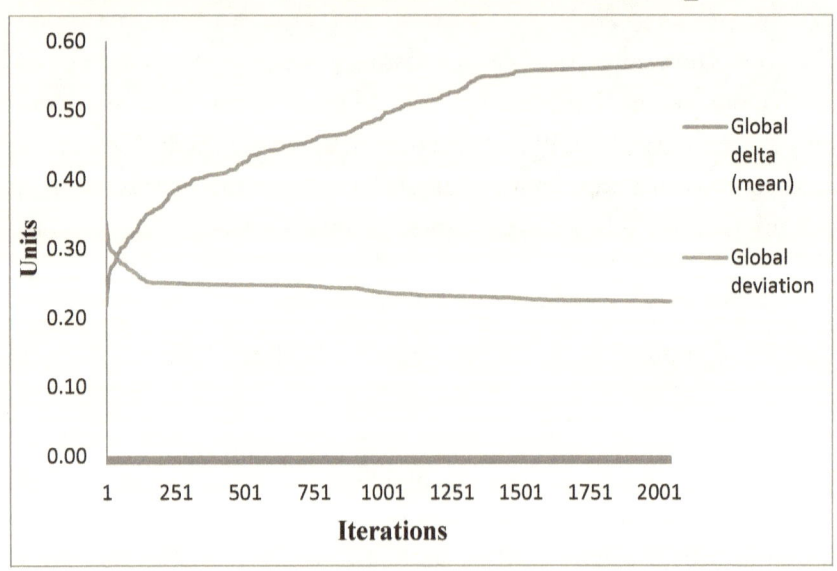

Source: Author, 2013 and 2021

Illustrations of the optimal solutions, adopting the knowledge interaction design criteria (KIDC) and the land-use cost criteria (LUCC), are depicted in Figures 4.8, 4.9, 4.10 and 4.11. Figure 4.8 depicts the developmental stage of the 'One North' KBUD by the institutional type of distribution. Figure 4.8 (a) and (b) captures the distribution of agents by institution and the knowledge base. Figure 4.9 (a) and (b) shows the land-use design split by the type of agents of the planned knowledge-based urban development (KBUD).

Figure 4.10 (a), (b) and (c) deploys the exported excel sheet of the detailed land-use design into the CityCad° software program or the three-dimensional representation of the baseline scenario. The detailed land-use plan, generated by the agent-based knowledge-based urban development-land use design model (KBUD-LUDM) for the One North knowledge based urban development (KBUD) baseline scenario, is provided in Appendix III for information and reference purposes.

Figure 4.11 presents the computer-aided design (CAD) model of the baseline agent-based model of the One North KBUD. subject to agent specification and in accordance with Tables 4.6 and 4.7. Figure 4.11's first image (a) gives an aerial view of the simulated three-dimensional models, showing the Biopolis and the Fusionopolis in the early Phase I of their development. Figure 4.11 (b) and (c) show a more detailed three-dimensional view and a street view of the Fusionopolis as seen from the nearby Biopolis. The green patches represent secondary agents, the green space distribution, while the red blocks are pre-existing institutional (educational and community) spaces. The grey patches (i.e. the rest) are undeveloped land parcels, ready for future urban development.

The Baseline Scenario successfully demonstrates the knowledge-based urban development-land use design model (KBUD-LUDM)'s ability, to replicate the first two phases of the One North KBUD. The KBUD-LUDM does not produce an exact replication of the One North KBUD, but a mere demonstration of the KBUD-LUDM's ability in attaining optimal land-use design solutions, via the agent-based modelling

(ABM) approach. As mentioned earlier, recall that the knowledge-based urban development-land use design model (KBUD-LUDM), is more a projection model rather than a prediction or a forecast model.

The Scenario Analysis

Alternative scenario planning is an integral part of the urban planning and development process. It helps stakeholders to realize the viability and flexibility of land-use design in times of uncertainty. The appropriate number of scenarios for urban planners is usually four to five. It is observed that some authors have noted that more than four to five scenarios, may confuse users, and may constrain the stakeholders ability to explore plausible uncertainties (Van der Heijden, 1996; Wack, 2002).

Scenario planning is conducted along a storyline approach, where at each stage of the planning process, the urban planner is required to enter an agent set i.e., the information on incoming actors and their rough proportions. The scenarios are broadly classified as the Optimistic, Pessimistic and Neutral Scenarios, reflecting the expected demand for space at the One North KBUD under different economic situations. Figure 4.12 depicts these three scenarios, as perceived by the knowledge-based urban development-land use design model (KBUD-LUDM).

Figure 4.12. The Scenario Thresholds for The One North KBUD-LUDM

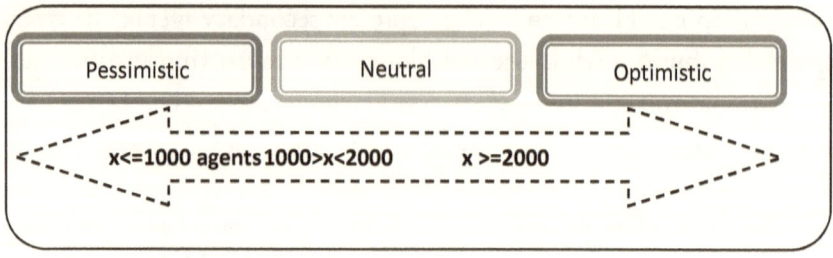

Source: Author, 2013 and 2021

Figure 4.8. Agent-Based Simulation of The Baseline Scenario of The One North KBUD (Institutional Color-Coded)

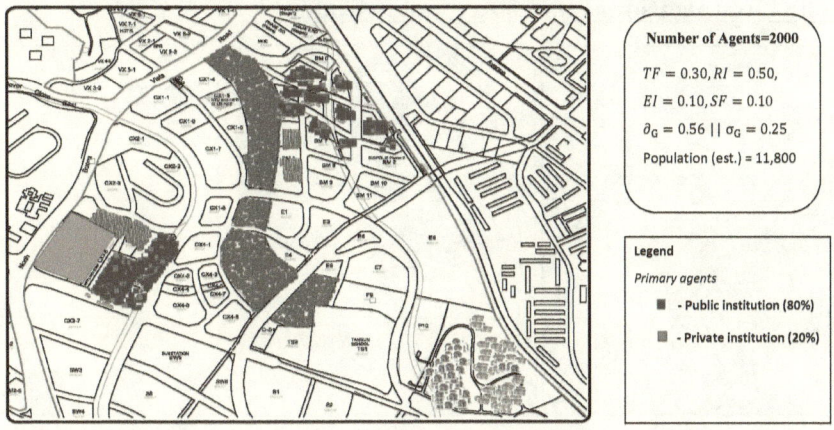

N.B. Figure 4.8 shows the optimal land-use design solution that maximises knowledge interactions for all agents based on knolwedge interaction design criteria (KIDC). The baseline shows the One north development arrested at Biopolis and Fusionopolis, which was the case at One north up till the year 2013. Source: Author, 2013 and 2021.

Figure 4.9. Agent-Based Simulation of The Baseline Scenario of One North By Agent Type (Primary And Secondary)

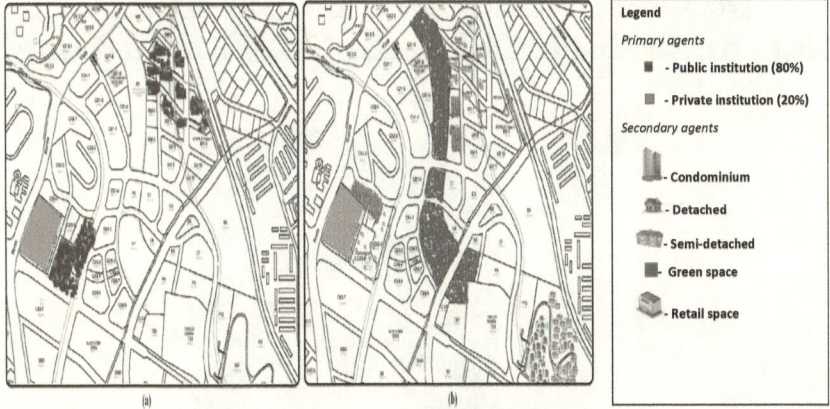

NB. In the previous Figure 4.8, the overlap of agents due to mixed-use zoning may cause difficulty in observing the different types of agents in the land-use design baseline scenario of One North. Figure 4.9 (a) and (b) shows the optimal land-use design solution, split by primary and secondary agents, respectively, for the baseline scenario. Source: Author, 2013 and 2021.

Figure 4.10. Agent-Based Simulation of The Baseline Scenario of The One North KBUD (Knowledge And The Organizational Bases Are Color Coded

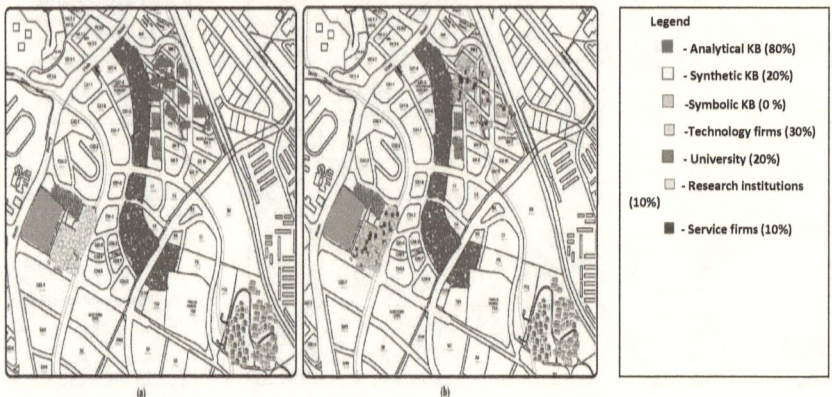

NB. Figure 4.10 (a) and (b) are similar to Figure 4.9. However, Figure 4.9 is colour-coded to illustrate the mix of (a) the knowledge bases and (b) the organisational bases, See legend on the right-hand side. Urban planners can derive zoning maps to indicate land parcels compatble with specific knowledge bases and organisational sectors within and between blocks, to facilitate the land-use design's overall knowledge interactions and consequently facilitate cross-fertilisation of ideas. Source: Author, 2013 and 2021

Figure 4.11. The Computer-Aided Design (CAD) Extension Of The Agent Based KBUD-LUDM) For The Baseline Scenario Of Singapore's One North KBUD Via The CitCad Software Program

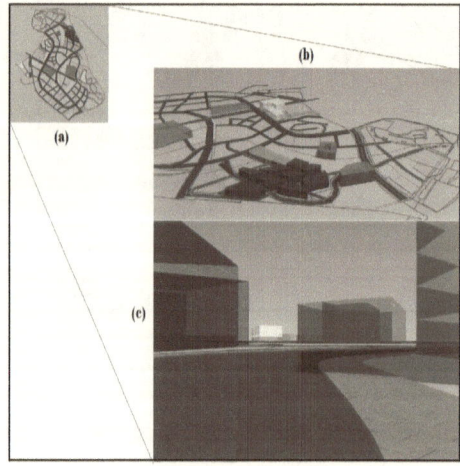

NB. Figure 4.11 represents the computer-aided design (CAD) model of the exported baseline agent-based model of the One North KBUD. subject to agent specification, in accordance with Tables 4.6 and 4.7. Figure 4.11's first image (a) gives an aerial view of the simulated three-dimensional models, showing the Biopolis and the Fusionopolis in their early stages of development (Phase I). Figure 4.11 (b) and (c) show a more detailed three-dimensional view and a street view of the Fusionopolis as seen from the nearby Biopolis. The green patches represent secondary agents, green space distribution, while the red blocks are pre-existing institutional (educational and community) spaces. The grey patches (i.e. the rest) are undeveloped land parcels, ready for future urban development. Source: Author, 2013 and 2021.

Table 4.8 showcases the set of input and output variables for a given set of scenarios. The first column shows the time horizon in years and the second column the scenario status (Optimistic, Neutral and Pessimistic). The first batch of the intake of tenants at the One North KBUD constitutes the Baseline Scenario and is deemed to be a successful scenario among Singapore urban planners. Figure 5.11 shows a evolutionary picture of the simulated knowledge-based urban development-land use design model (KBUD-LUDM) agent-based model simulations at every stage of the development process.

The frequency chosen for the scenario analysis is about three years; this gives the Knowledge-Based Urban Development-Land Use Design Model (KBUD-LUDM) an incremental planning approach as compared to One north's traditional masterplan of 30 years. The first scenario as shown in Table 5.8, which is right after the baseline scenario, and coincides with the periods after the recent financial crisis in Singapore. Therefore, urban planners in general expect a reduced demand for space for the next three years (2009–2012). Such a reduced demand phase is planned for only a fraction of the agents (~30%), as compared to the previous period (2003–2009). A total of 600 agents is expected to enter the knowledge-based urban development (KBUD).

The optimal design is obtained with a global delta (∂_G) of 0.45 and global sigma (σ_G) of 0.25, satisfying the knowledge interaction design criteria (KIDC), that is $0.30 >= \partial\_G <= 0.70$. In the first and second scenarios, the One North KBUD experiences an influx of the educational institutions and service firms; to support the existing technology firms and research institutions; to support knowledge production and to offer essential services respectively to the existing tenants.

Table 4.8. Results From the Knowledge-Based Urban Development-Land Use Design Model (KBUD-LUDM) For the Multiple Scenario Planning Approach

Time Horizon (In Years)	The Planning Scenario	Agent Initialization Procedure (AIP)				The KBUD-LUDM Outcome
		Number of agents per scenario	Agent Kb Ratio	Organizational type	Public-private ratio	Global delta ∂_G [sigma σ_Q]
2003-2009	Optimistic (baseline)	2000	α=0.5, β=0.5, γ=0	TF=0.30,RI=0.50, EI=0.10,SF=0.10	80:20	0.56 [0.25]
2012	Pessimistic	600	α=0.40, β=0.40, γ=0.20	TF=0.25,RI=0.45, EI=0.20,SF=0.10	70:30	0.45 [0.24]
2015	Pessimistic	1,000	α=0.30, β=0.30, γ=0.40	TF=0.20,RI=0.30, EI=0.15,SF=0.35	60:40	0.43 [0.19]
2018	Neutral	1,600	α=0.25, β=0.25, γ=0.50	TF=0.40,RI=0.10, EI=0.10,SF=0.40	50:50	0.49 [0.33]
2021	Optimistic	2,500	α=0.15, β=0.25, γ=0.60	TF=0.30,RI=0.30, EI=0.30,SF=0.10	40:60	0.46 [0.18]
2024	Optimistic	3,500	α=0.25, β=0.25, γ=0.50	TF=0.40,RI=0.15, EI=0.15,SF=0.30	30:70	0.31 [0.29]

NB. In Table 5.8, the α, β and γ represent the percentage of planned agents expected to belong to the analytical, synthetic and symbolic knowledge bases. The organizational types i.e. TF, RI, EI SF represent the expected percentages of the technology firms, research institutions, universities (educational) and the service firms. Source: Author, 2013 and 2021.

The first scenario of the One North KBUD also sees the launch of the Mediapolis cluster ($\gamma>0$), which is set to host the media-, design- and arts-related organisations. In the first phase of the Mediapolis, the initial demand for housing development (T1) begin. However, the Mediapolis does not fully occupy the available space on its site plot. The inference is that there can well be a waiting period till the critical population (>50%) is reached, to service the land. The second scenario slightly improves but remains in the Pessimistic Scenario, and with the demand for space being stifled owing to poor local and global economic conditions.

The third scenario sees the slow improvement of the economy, which switches into a Neutral Scenario with the inflow of actors to the Biopolis, Fusionopolis and Mediapolis clusters. This Neutral Scenario's Mediapolis cluster gains momentum by constituting a major proportion ($\gamma=0.50$) of the incoming actors. By now, the Biopolis and Fusionoplis clusters, constituting the north and west parts of their site, have each reached at least 60-70% land occupancy.

The fourth scenario switches to an Optimistic Scenario, and with rising demand for the Mediapolis and Fusionpolis, of which there is still availability of undeveloped land to be serviced. At this stage, a total of 10 condominium housing developments with a combined capacity 5,668 units accommodate families, which supports nearly 17,000 residents, is proposed for immediate development. Wessex Estate (in the southeast), which is zoned to host demi-detached and detached landed housing is slated for the development of 577 detached and 235 semi-detached landed housing, proposed to accommodate 3-4% of the total resident population.

Similarly, public sector participation is reduced as a proportion over the next four scenarios in Figure 4.12. This is in line with the Jurong Town Corporation (JTC)'s notion that public institutes (public participation in general) are to only provide an anchoring role for future private investments.

Figure 4.12. Expected Institutional Participation Levels Over Time in The Scenario Analysis

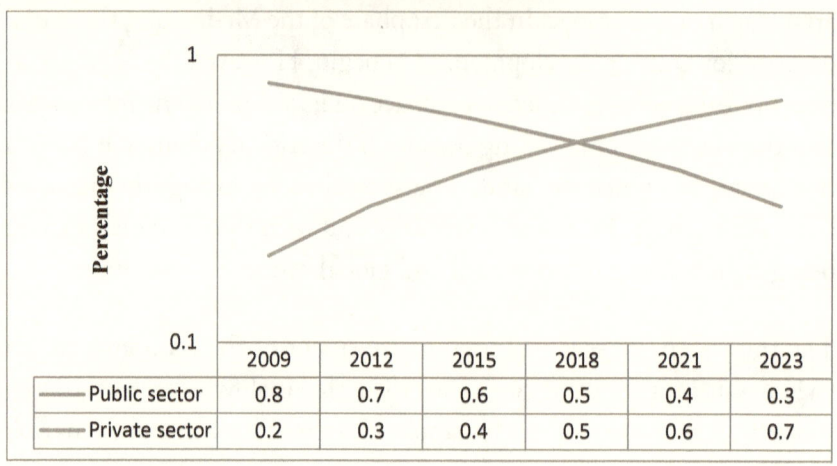

	2009	2012	2015	2018	2021	2023
——Public sector	0.8	0.7	0.6	0.5	0.4	0.3
——Private sector	0.2	0.3	0.4	0.5	0.6	0.7

Source: Author, 2013 and 2021

The fifth (last) scenario is expected to experience robust demand for space for all three clusters, owing to improved economic conditions. At this stage, the One North KBUD has a population of 121,640 with the percentage of built environment at just above 50%. Major site plots are proposed to be allocated for green spaces to compensate for the high presence of built-up spaces on site. Several land sites are deemed to be fit for housing development. Retail developments are incorporated as a percentage of every building to satisfy the minimum requirements as set out in Table 4.8. However and apart from the minimum requirements, then dedicated commercial and retail establishments are proposed for few land sites near the transit nodes.

Figure 4.13. depicts the evolution of the incremental planning of the One North knowledge based urban development (KBUD) into the future. Figure 4.13's simulation panels show the incremental planning approach for the One North knowledge based urban development (KBUD), in accordance with the AIP data of Table 4.6.

Figure 4.14 depicts the computer aided design (CAD) extension of the agent based KBUD-LUDM for the 'Final Scenario (2024)' of Singapore's One North KBUD, under the CityCad° software program. The blocks are representative of the One North KBUD's land development process up till the Baseline Scenario of Table 4.8. The purple blocks are the proposed blocks for development after all the five scenarios. The orange blocks are reserved for residential development. The red blocks represent existing institutional sites unavailable for development. The green strips represent land allocated for open spaces/parks, etc. The rest are undeveloped land available for future use of the One North KBUD.

Figure 4.13. Optimal Land Use Designs Obtained from The Scenario Analysis of the One North KBUD, Adopting The KBUD-LUDM

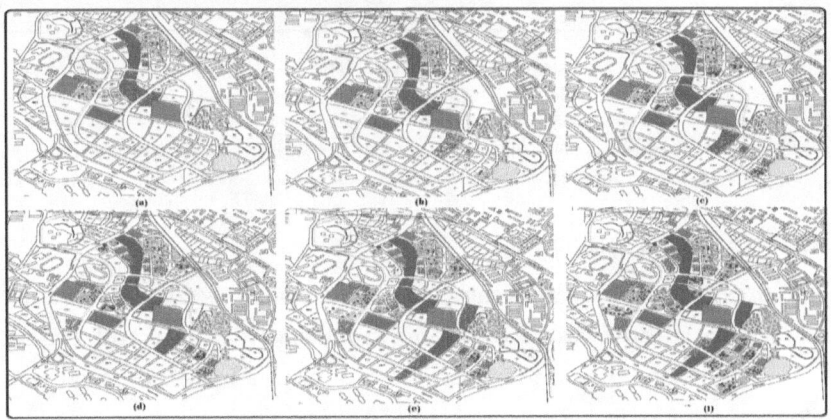

NB. The above simulation panels show the incremental planning approach for the One North knowledge based urban development (KBUD), in accordance with the AIP data given in Table 4.6. Source: Author, 2013 and 2021.

Figure 4.14. Computer Aided Design (CAD) Extension of The Agent Based KBUD-LUDM For The Final Scenario (2024) of Singapore's One North KBUD under The CityCad™ Program

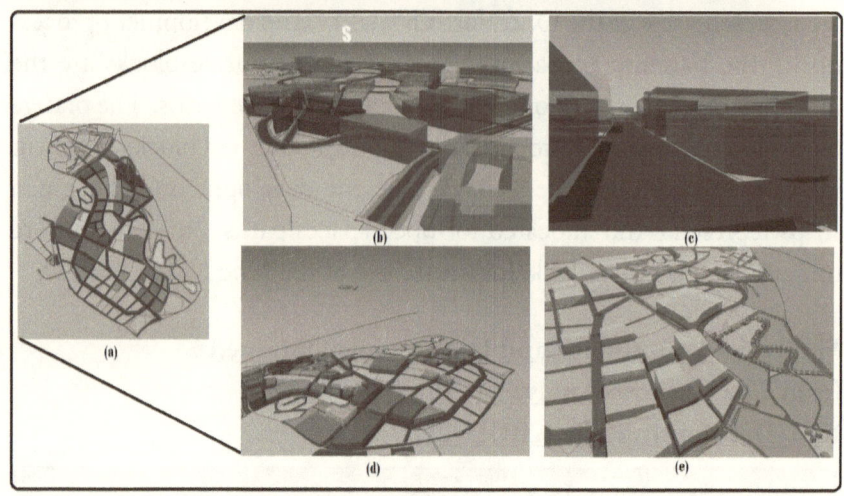

<u>NB</u>. The blue and yellow blocks are representative of One North KBUD's land development process up till the Baseline Scenario (see Table 4.8). The purple blocks are the proposed blocks for development after all five scenarios. The orange blocks are reserved for residential development. The red blocks represent existing institutional sites unavailable for development. The green strips represent land allocated for open spaces/parks etc. The rest are undeveloped land available for future use. Source: Author, 2013 and 2021.

The Validation procedure

The emergence of models in the agent-based modelling (ABM) literature has led to rising awareness among modelers, to check and correct for path dependency and multiple equilibrium issues, especially in economic, ecological and spatial land-use systems (Atkinson & Oleson, 1996; Balmann, 2001; Pahl-Wostl, 1995). Path dependency arises from negative and positive feedback that reinforce one another, to create large deviations from the optimal results. Therefore, there is growing necessity to validate spatial land-use models. Multiple equilibria is unfavorable because it increases the model's uncertainty, in obtaining the land use design solutions for planning purposes.

One can extend the foregoing concerns to a land-use design optimization model. Brown *et al.* (2005) suggest that modelers should focus on two aspects to validate the agent-based land-use models. The first aspect is to adopt *'aggregate similarity'*, to be followed by *'spatial similarity'*. For brevity, the rest of this discuss is moved to Appendix-IV. The complete validation procedure of the KBUD-LUDM is found therein.

Concluding Comments

City (urban) planners of the 21st century construe the knowledge-based urban development (KBUD) strategy to be a new form of urban renewal of the industrial cities. Many believe it potentially brings both economic prosperity and sustainable socio-spatial order to the contemporary city[10], as a positive force.

From the field work interviews and surveys of the case of the One North knowledge-based urban development (KBUD), there first appears to be a general lack of understanding about the actors of the KBUDs. Secondly, to what extent can the diversity of the actors concerned favor intra-cluster interactions? Therefore, further studies should look into the determinants of interaction between actors and their reliance on space requirements to facilitate them. The resultant ambiguity compels urban planners to explore 'interactive' environments, via physical planning (more specifically through mixed-use zoning), for the post-industrial cluster-based urban developments.

Thirdly, long-term land-use planning and design are becoming a less favorable option among urban planners, owing to rising land and urban development markets' volatility. The outcome is demand fluctuations, which jeopardize existing mixed-use design ratios and complimentary zoning. In other words, long-term traditional master planning is deemed to be simply too static for aiding the planning and development process of large-scale dynamic KBUDs for the 21st century.

Inefficient large-scale urban designs of planned post-industrial clusters have the potential to create the dissociation of related economic and

---

10   See Lee et al, (2008), T. Yigitcanlar, Velibeyoglu, et al. (2008)).

physical activities over space. Such uninformed urban designs can increase physical barriers between 'related' actors. Consequently, there would be a reduced level of intra-cluster knowledge interactions via planned and spontaneous channels. There would be much less vibrancy for the use of post-industrial spaces.

Several key questions can therefore be posed:

- Who are the actors of Knowledge-Based Urban Developments (KBUDs)?
- What is the theoretical urban design criterion that would maximize knowledge interaction among the participating actors?
- What is the optimal urban design of the Knowledge-Based Urban Development (KBUD), which enhances intra cluster knowledge interactions?
- How can we dynamically[11] design knowledge-based urban development (KBUD) systems?

The responses to the above questions are outlined herewith:

1) The actors of the KBUD comprise the primary and secondary agents. There are four generic actors, who participate in post-industrial clusters, namely, the technology firm (TF), the research institution (RI), the educational institution (EI) and finally the service firm (SF). Many post-industrial actors can be expressed as a combination of these primary agents. Secondary agents are supporting entities to the primary agents. The supporting activities can include the provision of green spaces, adequate housing, retail, commercial and recreational activities.
2) Well-planned mixed land use designs can help shape the knowledge-based interactions among the different types of actors. This can be achieved by placing 'related' workers near each other via complimentary zoning. A unique urban design criterion is suggested, which seeks to enhance the KBUD's knowledge interactions (KI).

---

11   Or incrementally.

Such a criterion can be used to identify 'related' actors if certain minimum information is available like the incoming participants in KBUD's. This criterion satisfies one of the three important rationales, adopted by urban planners when performing land-use zoning, to integrate compatible land uses, which generate positive externalities so that they are mutually beneficial. [12]

3) A knowledge interaction design criteria (KIDC) *is* proposed to obtain optimal land-use design solutions, via mixed-use zoning specifically for the KBUDs.

4) Agent-based modelling (ABM) is suggested as a dynamic methodology to handle spatial and temporal processes for land-use design optimization models, as compared to the simple and usual linear programming methodology that address land use design problems. A knowledge-based urban development-land use design model (KBUD-LUDM) is proposed that incorporate the knowledge interaction design criteria (KIDC). Such a model can be adopted for Singapore's One North KBUD, which demonstrates how urban planners can conduct incremental planning for long-term developments, like the KBUD via scenario planning and analysis.

5) Information and data on the environment and constraints for the KBUD-LUDM is sourced from the One North KBUD. The latter is an ideal case of the mixed-use development that aims to achieve intra-cluster interactions by accommodating a diversity of actors and activities. The agent-based model output produces two-dimensional land use maps an even three-dimensional block diagrams, via computer aided design (CAD).

It is well known among urban planning professionals that long-term designs are too static to cater to dynamic environments like the KBUD. The inherent problem is the flight of labor and capital that the KBUD faces, owing to the forces of globalization. On future studies, rational planning models like

---

12   The other two rationales are (2) separating incompatible uses that generate negative externalities and (3) interjecting public goods like roads and open space to improve social welfare (environmental benefits).

the knowledge-based urban development-land use design model (KBUD-LUDM) can be extended to enhance its direct applicability to other case studies, apart from the One North KBUD. From Figure 4.15., the KBUD-LUDM adopts only two criteria, namely, the knowledge interaction design criteria (KIDC) and the land-use cost criteria (LUCC).

For better integration of the two-dimensional and the three-dimensional outputs, the latest versions of the agent-based modelling (ABM) software program offer in-built three-dimensional modelling support. As such, there is no need to deploy any external computer-aided design (CAD) program. It may well be more efficient, be saving on operational time, and to potentially enhance the urban planner's engagement with the public at large, during the consultative planning process.

Figure 4.15. The Agent Based KBUD-LUDM, The KIDC & The LUCC

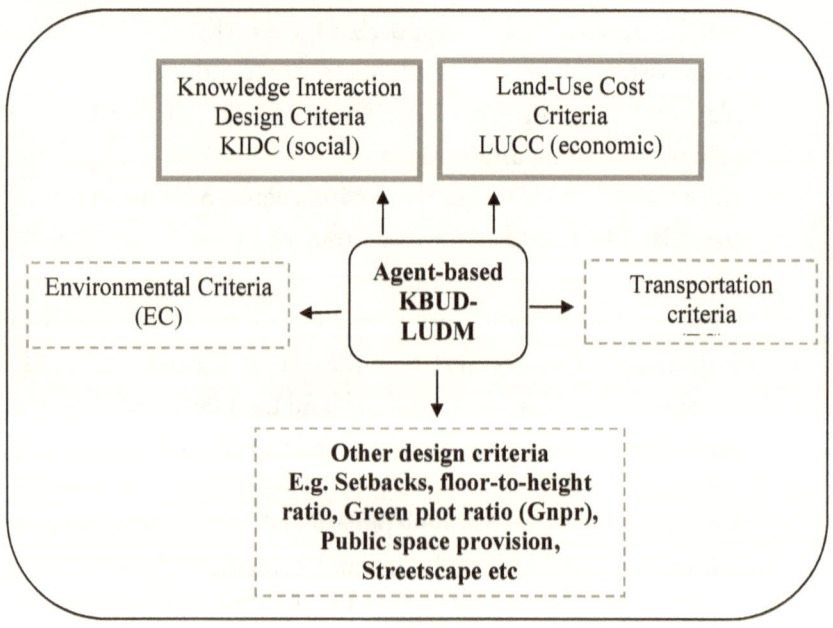

Source: Author, 2021

(The author wishes to acknowledge his appreciation to Dr Rengarajan Satyanarain, a former NUS research scholar, and now a management information system consultant; for his meaningful contribution and perseverance in sourcing the related literature, the required primary data and for the initial analysis).

References

Abukhater, A. B. E.-D. (2009). Rethinking planning theory and practice: a glimmer of light for Prospects of integrated planning to combat complex urban realities. *Theoretical and Empirical Researches in Urban Management, 4*(2 (11)), 64-79.

Acs, Z. J., & Audretsch, D. B. (1990). *Innovation Ans Small Firms*: The MIT Press.

Allen, T. J. (1984). Managing the flow of technology: Technology transfer and the dissemination of technological information within the R&D organization. *MIT Press Books, 1*.

Ancona, D. G., & Caldwell, D. F. (1992). Bridging the boundary: External activity and performance in organizational teams. *Administrative science quarterly*, 634-665.

Anselin, L., Varga, A., & Acs, Z. (1997). Local geographic spillovers between university research and high technology innovations. *Journal of Urban Economics, 42*(3), 422-448.

Antonelli, C. (2000). New information technology and localized technological change in the knowledge-based economy. *Services and the Knowledge-Based Economy. Continuum. London and New York*.

Arad, R. W., & Berechman, J. (1978). A design model for allocating interrelated land-use activities in discrete space. *Environment and Planning A, 10*(11), 1319-1332.

Asheim, & Gertler, M. (2005). The geography of innovation. *The Oxford handbook of innovation*, 291-317.

Asheim, B., Coenen, L., & Vang, J. (2007). Face-to-face, buzz, and knowledge bases: sociospatial implications for learning, innovation, and innovation policy. *Environment and Planning C, 25*(5), 655.

Asheim, B. T., & Clark, G. (2000). Industrial districts: the contributions of Marshall and beyond. *The Oxford handbook of economic geography*, 413-431.

Atkinson, G., & Oleson, T. (1996). Urban sprawl as a path dependent process. *Journal of Economic Issues*, 609-615.

Audretsch, D. B., & Feldman, M. P. (1996). R&D spillovers and the geography of innovation and production. *The American Economic Review, 86*(3), 630-640.

Axtell, R. L., Epstein, J. M., Dean, J. S., Gumerman, G. J., Swedlund, A. C., Harburger, J., . . . Parker, M. (2002). Population growth and collapse in a multiagent model of the Kayenta Anasazi in Long House Valley. *Proceedings of the National Academy of Sciences of the United States of America, 99*(Suppl 3), 7275-7279. doi: 10.1073/pnas.092080799

Bajracharya, B., Too, L., Imukuka, J., & Hearn, G. (2009). *Developing knowledge precincts in regional towns: Opportunities and challenges.* Paper presented at the 2nd International Urban Design Conference (Gold Coast, Australia.

Bajracharya, B., & Too, L. I., J. . (2009). Developing Knowledge Precincts in Regional Towns: Opportunities and Challenges. *paper presented at the 2nd International Urban Design.*

Balmann, A. (2001). Modeling Land Use with Multi-agent Systems: Perspectives for the Analyis of Agricultural Policies.

Bania, N., Calkins, L. N., & Dalenberg, D. R. (1992). THE EFFECTS OF REGIONAL SCIENCE AND TECHNOLOGY POLICY ON THE GEOGRAPHIC DISTRIBUTION OF

INDUSTRIAL R&D LABORATORIES*. *Journal of Regional Science, 32*(2), 209-228.

Baptista, R., & Swann, P. (1998). Do firms in clusters innovate more? *Research Policy, 27*(5), 525-540.

Barber, G. (1976). Land-use plan design via interactive multiple-objective programming. *Environment and Planning A, 8*(6), 625-636.

Bathelt, H., Malmberg, A., & Maskell, P. (2004). Clusters and knowledge: local buzz, global pipelines and the process of knowledge creation. *Progress in Human geography, 28*(1), 31-56.

Batty, M. (2003). Agent-based pedestrian modelling. *Advanced spatial analysis: The CASA book of GIS*, 81-106.

Batty, M. (2005). Agents, cells, and cities: new representational models for simulating multiscale urban dynamics.

Batty, M., Chapman, D., Evans, S., Haklay, M., Kueppers, S., Shiode, N., . . . Torrens, P. M. (2000). Visualizing the city: communicating urban design to planners and decision-makers.

Batty, M., & Longley, P. (1994). Fractal cities: a geometry of form and function.

Black, D., & Henderson, V. (2003). Urban Evolution in the USA. *Journal of economic geography, 3*(4), 343-372.

Boschma, R. (2005). Proximity and innovation: a critical assessment. *Regional studies, 39*(1), 61-74.

Bottazzi, L., & Peri, G. (2003). Innovation and spillovers in regions: Evidence from European patent data. *European Economic Review, 47*(4), 687-710.

Breschi, S., & Lissoni, F. (2001). Localised knowledge spillovers vs. innovative milieux: Knowledge "tacitness" reconsidered. *Papers in regional science, 80*(3), 255-273.

Brown, D. G., Page, S., Riolo, R., Zellner, M., & Rand, W. (2005). Path dependence and the validation of agent-based spatial models of land use. *International Journal of Geographical Information Science, 19*(2), 153-174.

Brown, M., Falk, A., & Fehr, E. (2004). Relational contracts and the nature of market interactions. *Econometrica, 72*(3), 747-780.

Camagni, R. (1991). *Innovation networks*: John Wiley & Sons, Inc.

Cantwell, J., & Santangelo, G. D. (2003). The new geography of corporate research in information and communications technology (ICT) *Change, Transformation and Development* (pp. 343-377): Springer.

Capello, R., & Faggian, A. (2005). Collective learning and relational capital in local innovation processes. *Regional studies, 39*(1), 75-87.

Carrillo, F. J. (2004). Capital cities: a taxonomy of capital accounts for knowledge cities. *Journal of Knowledge Management, 8*(5), 28-46.

Carsjens, G. J., van Lammeren, R. J., & Ligtenberg, A. (2003). STEPP: A strategic tool for integrating environmental aspects into planning procedures *Planning Support Systems in Practice* (pp. 139-154): Springer.

Castells, M., & Borja, J. (1998). *Local y global*: Taurus.

Castells, M., & Hall, P. (2009). Technopoles of the world: The making of twenty-first-century industrial complexes.

Cetin, N., Burri, A., & Nagel, K. (2003). *A large-scale agent-based traffic microsimulation based on queue model.* Paper presented at the IN PROCEEDINGS OF SWISS TRANSPORT RESEARCH CONFERENCE (STRC), MONTE VERITA, CH.

Chatterji, A., Glaeser, E. L., & Kerr, W. R. (2013). Clusters of Entrepreneurship and Innovation: National Bureau of Economic Research.

Chatzkel, J. (2004). Greater Phoenix as a knowledge capital. *Journal of Knowledge Management, 8*(5), 61-72.

Chen, X., & Zhan, F. B. (2006). Agent-based modelling and simulation of urban evacuation: relative effectiveness of simultaneous and staged evacuation strategies. *Journal of the Operational Research Society, 59*(1), 25-33.

Cheng, P., Choi, C. J., Chen, S., Eldomiaty, T. I., & Millar, C. C. (2004). Knowledge repositories in knowledge cities: institutions, conventions and knowledge subnetworks. *Journal of Knowledge Management, 8*(5), 96-106.

Chung, L. L. W. (1994). The economics of land-use zoning: a literature review and analysis of the work of Coase. *Town planning review, 65*(1), 77.

Clark, J. S., Carpenter, S. R., Barber, M., Collins, S., Dobson, A., Foley, J. A., . . . Pizer, W. (2001). Ecological forecasts: an emerging imperative. *Science, 293*(5530), 657-660.

Cohen, W. M., & Levinthal, D. A. (1990). Absorptive capacity: a new perspective on learning and innovation. *Administrative science quarterly,* 128-152.

Cooke, P. (2001). Regional innovation systems, clusters, and the knowledge economy. *Industrial and corporate change, 10*(4), 945-974.

Cooke, P., Uranga, M. G., & Etxebarria, G. (1998). Regional systems of innovation: an evolutionary perspective. *Environment and Planning A, 30*, 1563-1584.

Coombs, R., Narandren, P., & Richards, A. (1996). A literature-based innovation output indicator. *Research Policy, 25*(3), 403-413.

Corey, K. E., & Wilson, M. (2006). *Urban and regional technology planning: planning practice in the global knowledge economy* (Vol. 3): Routledge.

Correia, P., & Madden, M. (1985). Optimisation of land purchasing and management using mixed integer programming: a case study in a Portuguese municipal authority. *Environment and Planning B: Planning and Design, 12*(3), 335-349.

David, P. A., & Foray, D. (2003). Economic fundamentals of the knowledge society. *Policy Futures in Education, Volume 1*.

Davidoff, P. (1965). Advocacy and pluralism in planning. *Journal of the American Institute of Planners, 31*(4), 331-338.

Davis, J., & Grant, I. (1987). ADAPT: a knowledge-based decision support system for producing zoning schemes. *Environment and Planning B: Planning and Design, 14*(1), 53-66.

De Meyer, A. (1991). Organizational leverage effect in innovation. *European Management Journal, 9*(4), 397-403.

Deadman, P., & Gimblett, R. H. (1994). A role for goal-oriented autonomous agents in modeling people-environment interactions in forest recreation. *Mathematical and Computer Modelling, 20*(8), 121-133.

Deadman, P. J. (1999). Modelling individual behaviour and group performance in an intelligent agent-based simulation of the tragedy of the commons. *Journal of Environmental Management, 56*(3), 159-172.

den Hertog, P. (2002). 10. Co-producers of innovation: on the role of knowledge-intensive business services in innovation. *Productivity, innovation and knowledge in services: New economic and socio-economic approaches*, 223.

Diamond, J. T., & Wright, J. R. (1988). Design of an integrated spatial information system for multiobjective land-use planning. *Environment and Planning B, 15*(2), 205-214.

Dresner, K., & Stone, P. (2004). *Multiagent traffic management: A reservation-based intersection control mechanism*. Paper presented at the Proceedings of the Third International Joint Conference on Autonomous Agents and Multiagent Systems-Volume 2.

Duffy, F. (1997). The new office. *London, Conran Octopus*.

Duffy, F., Jaunzens, D., Laing, A., & Willis, S. (2012). *New environments for working*: Taylor & Francis.

Duijn, M., Immers, L., Waaldijk, F., & Stoelhorst, H. (2003). Gaming Approach Route 26: a combination of computer simulation, design tools and social interaction. *Journal of Artificial Societies and Social Simulation, 6*(3).

Dvir, R. (2006). Knowledge city, seen as a collage of human knowledge moments. *Knowledge Cities: Approaches, Experiences, and Perspectives. Amsterdam, Boston, Heldelberg, London, New York, Oxford, Paris, San Diego, San Francisco, Singapore, Sydney, Tokyo: Elsevier*, 245-272.

Dvir, R., & Pasher, E. (2004). Innovation engines for knowledge cities: an innovation ecology perspective. *Journal of Knowledge Management, 8*(5), 16-27.

EDB. (2013). Biopolis, Fusionopolis, Mediapolis. Retrieved December, 2013

Edquist, C., & Johnson, B. (1997). *Institutions and organizations in systems of innovation*: Univ.

Elfring, T., & Hulsink, W. (2003). Networks in entrepreneurship: the case of high-technology firms. *Small business economics, 21*(4), 409-422.

Epstein, J. M. (2006). *Generative social science: Studies in agent-based computational modeling*: Princeton University Press.

Ergazakis, K., Metaxiotis, K., & Psarras, J. (2006). *An emerging pattern of successful knowledge cities' main features*: Elsevier, Amsterdam.

Etzkowitz, H., & Leydesdorff, L. (2000). The dynamics of innovation: from National Systems and "Mode 2" to a Triple Helix of university–industry–government relations. *Research Policy, 29*(2), 109-123.

Eubank, S., Guclu, H., Kumar, V. A., Marathe, M. V., Srinivasan, A., Toroczkai, Z., & Wang, N. (2004). Modelling disease outbreaks in realistic urban social networks. *Nature, 429*(6988), 180-184.

Feldman, M. P. (1994). *The geography of innovation* (Vol. 2): Springer.

Feldman, M. P. (1999). The new economics of innovation, spillovers and agglomeration: A review of empirical studies. *Economics of innovation and new technology, 8*(1-2), 5-25.

Felsenstein, D. (1994). University-related science parks—'seedbeds' or 'enclaves' of innovation? *Technovation, 14*(2), 93-110.

Foray, D. (2005). Economic fundamentals of the knowledge society. *Informationsgesellschaft. Geschichten und Wirklichkeit. Fribourg. S,* 211-240.

Fox, M. S., Barbuceanu, M., & Teigen, R. (2000). Agent-oriented supply-chain management. *International Journal of Flexible Manufacturing Systems, 12*(2-3), 165-188.

Freeman, C., & Soete, L. L. (1997). *The economics of industrial innovation*: Routledge.

Fritsch, M., & Schwirten, C. (1999). Enterprise-university co-operation and the role of public research institutions in regional innovation systems. *Industry and Innovation, 6*(1), 69-83.

Gadrey, J., Gallouj, F., & Weinstein, O. (1995). New modes of innovation: how services benefit industry. *International journal of service industry management, 6*(3), 4-16.

Garcia, B. C. (2004). Developing futures: a knowledge-based capital for Manchester. *Journal of Knowledge Management, 8*(5), 47-60.

García, B. C. (2006). UniverCities: innovation and social capital in Greater Manchester. *Knowledge Cities: Approaches, Experiences, and Perspectives*, 123-134.

Geertman, S., & Stillwell, J. (2004). Planning support systems: an inventory of current practice. *Computers, Environment and Urban Systems, 28*(4), 291-310.

Gibbs, D., & Deutz, P. (2005). Implementing industrial ecology? Planning for eco-industrial parks in the USA. *Geoforum, 36*(4), 452-464.

Gilbert, N., & Terna, P. (2000). How to build and use agent-based models in social science. *Mind & Society, 1*(1), 57-72.

Gordon, I. R., & McCann, P. (2000). Industrial clusters: complexes, agglomeration and/or social networks? *Urban Studies, 37*(3), 513-532.

Greenstone, M., & Looney, A. (2010). *An economic strategy to renew American communities*: Hamilton Project, Brookings Institution.

Hannan, M. T., & Freeman, J. (1977). The population ecology of organizations. *American journal of sociology*, 929-964.

Hargadon, A., & Sutton, R. I. (1997). Technology brokering and innovation in a product development firm. *Administrative science quarterly*, 716-749.

Harris, B. (1967). THE CITY OF THE FUTURE: THE PROBLEM OF OPTIMAL DESIGN. *Papers in regional science, 19*(1), 185-195. doi: 10.1111/j.1435-5597.1967.tb01377.x

Hegselmann, R., & Flache, A. (1998). Understanding complex social dynamics: A plea for cellular automata based modelling. *Journal of Artificial Societies and Social Simulation, 1*(3), 1.

Henderson, J. V. (2003). Marshall's scale economies. *Journal of Urban Economics, 53*(1), 1-28.

Henrekson, M. (2005). Entrepreneurship: a weak link in the welfare state? *Industrial and corporate change, 14*(3), 437-467.

Hertog, P. d. (2000). Knowledge-intensive business services as co-producers of innovation. *International Journal of Innovation Management, 4*(04), 491-528.

Hilferink, M., & Rietveld, P. (1999). Land Use Scanner: An integrated GIS based model for long term projections of land use in urban and rural areas. *Journal of Geographical Systems, 1*(2), 155-177.

Hillier, B., O'Sullivan, P., Penn, A., Kolokotroni, M., Rasmussen, M., & Xu, J. (1990). The design of research laboratories.

Hobday, M. (1988). Innovation and market structure: Lessons from the computer and semiconductor industries: Nancy S. Dorfman,(Harper and Row, New York, 1986) pp. 263: North-Holland.

Hoppenbrouwer, E., & Louw, E. (2005). Mixed-use development: Theory and practice in Amsterdam's Eastern Docklands. *European Planning Studies, 13*(7), 967-983.

Hughes, H. P., Clegg, C. W., Robinson, M. A., & Crowder, R. M. (2012). Agent-based modelling and simulation: The potential contribution to organizational psychology. *Journal of Occupational and Organizational Psychology, 85*(3), 487-502.

Isaksen, A. (2004). Knowledge-based clusters and urban location: the clustering of software consultancy in Oslo. *Urban Studies, 41*(5-6), 1157-1174.

Jaffe, A. B., Trajtenberg, M., & Henderson, R. (1993). Geographic localization of knowledge spillovers as evidenced by patent citations. *the Quarterly journal of Economics, 108*(3), 577-598.

Janssen, R., van Herwijnen, M., Stewart, T. J., & Aerts, J. (2008). Multiobjective decision support for land-use planning. *ENVIRONMENT AND PLANNING B PLANNING AND DESIGN, 35*(4), 740.

Ji-ci, W. (2004). DEVELOPING INNOVATION-BASED INDUSTRIAL CLUSTERS: POLICY RECOMMENDATIONS [J]. *Economic Geography, 4,* 001.

JTC. (2010). *JTC official statistics and design guidlines of One north development (Masterplan). Singapore: Jurong Town Corporation. (private).*

Kaasa, A. (2009). Effects of different dimensions of social capital on innovative activity: Evidence from Europe at the regional level. *Technovation, 29*(3), 218-233.

Kanter, R. M. (1988). Three tiers for innovation research. *Communication Research, 15*(5), 509-523.

Kesidou, E., Caniëls, M. C., & Romijn, H. A. (2009). Local Knowledge Spillovers and Development: An Exploration of the Software Cluster in Uruguay: Research Paper. *Industry and Innovation, 16*(2), 247-272.

Knaap, G. J., Hopkins, L. D., & Donaghy, K. P. (1998). Do plans matter? A game-theoretic model for examining the logic and effects of land use planning. *Journal of Planning Education and Research, 18*(1), 25-34.

Knight, R. V. (1973). Employment Expansion and Metropolitan Trade.

Knight, R. V. (1995). Knowledge-based development: policy and planning implications for cities. *Urban Studies, 32*(2), 225-260.

Knoben, J., & Oerlemans, L. A. G. (2006). Proximity and inter-organizational collaboration: A literature review. *International Journal of Management Reviews, 8*(2), 71-89. doi: 10.1111/j.1468-2370.2006.00121.x

Koh, F. C., Koh, W. T., & Tschang, F. T. (2005). An analytical framework for science parks and technology districts with an application to Singapore. *Journal of Business Venturing, 20*(2), 217-239.

Kolko, J. (2007). Can I Get Some Service Here? Information Technology, Service Industries, and the Future of Cities. *Information Technology, Service Industries, and the Future of Cities (November 1999)*.

Krugman, P. R. (1991). *Geography and trade*: MIT press.

Lawson, C., & Lorenz, E. (1999). Collective learning, tacit knowledge and regional innovative capacity. *Regional studies, 33*(4), 305-317.

Levitt, B., & March, J. G. (1988). Organizational learning. *Annual review of sociology*, 319-340.

Leyden, K. M. (2003). Social capital and the built environment: the importance of walkable neighborhoods. *American journal of public health, 93*(9), 1546-1551.

Leydesdorff, L., & Etzkowitz, H. (1996). Emergence of a Triple Helix of university—industry—government relations. *Science and public policy, 23*(5), 279-286.

Ligmann-Zielinska, A., & Jankowski, P. (2007). Agent-based models as laboratories for spatially explicit planning policies. *Environment and Planning B: Planning and Design, 34*(2), 316-335.

Ligtenberg, A., Beulens, A., Kettenis, D., Bregt, A. K., & Wachowicz, M. (2009). Simulating knowledge sharing in spatial planning: an agent-based approach. *Environment and planning. B, Planning & design, 36*(4), 644.

Ligtenberg, A., Wachowicz, M., Bregt, A. K., Beulens, A., & Kettenis, D. L. (2004). A design and application of a multi-agent system for simulation of multi-actor spatial planning. *Journal of Environmental Management, 72*(1), 43-55.

Lundvall, B.-Ä., & Johnson, B. (1994). The learning economy. *Journal of industry studies, 1*(2), 23-42.

Lundvall, B. (1985). Product Innovation. *Interactive Learning and Economic Performance.*

Lundvall, B., & Johnson, B. (1994). The learning economy. *Journal of industry studies, 1*(2), 23-42.

Lundvall, B. Ä., & Johnson, B. Ä. (1994). The learning economy. *Journal of industry studies, 1*(2), 23-42.

Makowski, D., Hendrix, E. M., van Ittersum, M. K., & Rossing, W. A. (2000). A framework to study nearly optimal solutions of linear programming models developed for agricultural land use exploration. *Ecological Modelling, 131*(1), 65-77.

Makse, H. A., Andrade, J. S., Batty, M., Havlin, S., & Stanley, H. E. (1998). Modeling urban growth patterns with correlated percolation. *Physical Review E, 58*(6), 7054.

Malecki, E. (1997). Technology and economic development: the dynamics of local, regional, and national change. *University of Illinois at Urbana-Champaign's Academy for Entrepreneurial Leadership Historical Research Reference in Entrepreneurship.*

Malmberg, A., & Maskell, P. (2006). Localized learning revisited. *Growth and Change, 37*(1), 1-18.

Markusen, A. (1999). Fuzzy concepts, scanty evidence, policy distance: the case for rigour and policy relevance in critical regional studies. *Regional studies, 33*(9), 869-884.

Marshall, A. (1920). Principles of economics: an introductory volume.

Mascitelli, R. (2000). From experience: harnessing tacit knowledge to achieve breakthrough innovation. *Journal of product innovation management, 17*(3), 179-193.

Meeus, M., Oerlemans, L., & Hage, J. (2004). Industry-public knowledge infrastructure interaction: intra-and inter-organizational explanations of interactive learning. *Industry and Innovation, 11*(4), 327-352.

Mommaas, H. (2004). Cultural clusters and the post-industrial city: towards the remapping of urban cultural policy. *Urban Studies, 41*(3), 507-532.

Moodysson, J., Coenen, L., & Asheim, B. (2008). Explaining spatial patterns of innovation: analytical and synthetic modes of knowledge creation in the Medicon Valley life-science cluster. *Environment and Planning A, 40*(5), 1040-1056.

Moulin, B., Chaker, W., & Gancet, J. (2004). PADI-Simul: an agent-based geosimulation software supporting the design of geographic spaces. *Computers, Environment and Urban Systems, 28*(4), 387-420. doi: http://dx.doi.org/10.1016/S0198-9715(03)00063-2

Muller, E., & Zenker, A. (2001a). Business services as actors of knowledge transformation: the role of KIBS in regional and national innovation systems. *Research Policy, 30*(9), 2.

Muller, E., & Zenker, A. (2001b). Business services as actors of knowledge transformation: the role of KIBS in regional and national innovation systems. *Research Policy, 30*(9), 1501-1516.

Nelson, R. R. (1986). Institutions supporting technical advance in industry. *The American Economic Review, 76*(2), 186-189.

Niu, X., McCalla, G., & Vassileva, J. (2003). Purpose-based user modelling in a multi-agent portfolio management system *User Modeling 2003* (pp. 398-402): Springer.

Nonaka, I., & Konno, N. (1998). Intellectualizing capability. *Knowledge Management.*

Nonaka, I., & Takeuchi, H. (1995). *The knowledge-creating company: How Japanese companies create the dynamics of innovation*: Oxford University Press, USA.

North, D. C. (1990). *Institutions, institutional change and economic performance*: Cambridge university press.

OECD. (2000). 21ˢᵗ Century Learning: Research, Innovation and Policy. *Directions from recent OECD analyses. Centre for Educational Reasearch and Innovation (CERI).*

Opdam, P., Steingröver, E., & Rooij, S. v. (2006). Ecological networks: a spatial concept for multi-actor planning of sustainable landscapes. *Landscape and urban planning, 75*(3), 322-332.

Pahl-Wostl, C. (1995). *The dynamic nature of ecosystems: chaos and order entwined*: Wiley Chichester.

Parayil, G. (2005). From" silicon island" to" biopolis of Asia": Innovation policy and shifting competitive strategy in Singapore. *California Management Review, 47*(2), 50-+.

Pavitt, K. (1984). Sectoral patterns of technical change: towards a taxonomy and a theory. *Research Policy, 13*(6), 343-373.

Pavitt, K. (1987). The objectives of technology policy. *Science and public policy, 14*(4), 182-188.

Penn, A., & Hillier, B. (1992). The social potential of buildings: spatial structure and the innovative millieu in scientific research laboratories.

Peterson, G. D., Cumming, G. S., & Carpenter, S. R. (2003). Scenario planning: a tool for conservation in an uncertain world. *Conservation biology, 17*(2), 358-366.

Pouder, R., & St. John, C. H. (1996). Hot spots and blind spots: geographical clusters of firms and innovation. *Academy of Management Review*, 1192-1225.

Powell, W. W., & Snellman, K. (2004). The knowledge economy. *Annual review of sociology*, 199-220.

Power, D., & Jansson, J. (2004). The emergence of a post-industrial music economy? Music and ICT synergies in Stockholm, Sweden. *Geoforum, 35*(4), 425-439.

Rashid, M., Kampschroer, K., & Zimring, C. (2006). Spatial layout and face-to-face interaction in offices-a study of the mechanisms of spatial effects on face-to-face interaction. *ENVIRONMENT AND PLANNING B PLANNING AND DESIGN, 33*(6), 825.

Rees, J., & Stafford, H. A. (1986). Location: their relevance for understanding high-technology complexes. *Technology, regions, and policy*, 23.

Roelandt, T. J., & Den Hertog, P. (1999). Cluster analysis and cluster-based policy making in OECD countries: an introduction to the theme. *Boosting innovation: The cluster approach*, 9-23.

Rowley, A. (1996). Mixed-use development: ambiguous concept, simplistic analysis and wishful thinking? *Planning Practice and Research, 11*(1), 85-98.

Said, L. B., Bouron, T., & Drogoul, A. (2002). *Agent-based interaction analysis of consumer behavior.* Paper presented at the Proceedings of the first international joint conference on Autonomous agents and multiagent systems: part 1.

Salter, A., & Gann, D. (2003). Sources of ideas for innovation in engineering design. *Research Policy, 32*(8), 1309-1324.

Sarimin, M., & Yigitcanlar, T. (2011). Knowledge-based urban development of Multimedia Super Corridor, Malaysia: an overview. *International Journal of Knowledge-Based Development, 2*(1), 34-48.

Saxenian, A. (1994). Regional networks: industrial adaptation in Silicon Valley and route 128. *Cityscape: a Journal of Policy Development and Research, 2*.

Saxenian, A. (1996). *Regional advantage: Culture and competition in Silicon Valley and Route 128*: Harvard University Press.

Schlager, K. J. (1965). A land use plan design model. *Journal of the American Institute of Planners, 31*(2), 103-111.

Schmitz, H. (1999). Collective efficiency and increasing returns. *Cambridge Journal of Economics, 23*(4), 465-483.

Scott, J. C. (1998). *Seeing like a state: How certain schemes to improve the human condition have failed*: Yale University Press.

Searle, G., & Pritchard, B. (2008). Beyond planning: Sydney's knowledge sector development.

Segal, N. S., Smilor, R., Kozmetsky, G., & Gibson, D. (1988). The Cambridge Phenomenon: universities, research, and local economic development in Great Britain. *Creating the Technopolis. Ballinger, Cambridge (Massachusetts)*, 81-90.

Shaw, A. T., & Gilly, J.-P. (2000). On the analytical dimension of proximity dynamics. *Regional studies, 34*(2), 169-180.

Simon, H. A. (1955). A behavioral model of rational choice. *the Quarterly journal of Economics, 69*(1), 99-118.

Simon, H. A. (1996). *The sciences of the artificial*: MIT press.

Smilor, R. W., Kozmetsky, G., & Gibson, D. V. (1987). *The Austin/San Antonio corridor: the dynamics of a developing technopolis*: IC2 Institute, University of Texas at Austin.

Smith, K. G., Collins, C. J., & Clark, K. D. (2005). Existing knowledge, knowledge creation capability, and the rate of new product introduction in high-technology firms. *Academy of management Journal, 48*(2), 346-357.

Sonnenwald, D. H. (1999). *Evolving perspectives of human information behavior: Contexts, situations, social networks and information horizons.* Paper presented at the Exploring the contexts of information behavior: Proceedings of the Second International Conference in Information Needs.

Stanback, T. M., & Knight, R. V. (1970). *The metropolitan economy: the process of employment expansion*: Columbia University Press New York.

Stewart, A. (2001). The Conversing Company – Its Power, Culture and Potential. *presented at the 1st world conference of systematic management, Vienna.*

Tödtling, F., Lehner, P., & Trippl, M. (2006). Innovation in knowledge intensive industries: The nature and geography of knowledge links. *European Planning Studies, 14*(8), 1035-1058. doi: 10.1080/09654310600852365

Toker, U., & Gray, D. O. (2008). Innovation spaces: Workspace planning and innovation in US university research centers. *Research Policy, 37*(2), 309-329.

Torre, A., & Rallet, A. (2005). Proximity and localization. *Regional studies, 39*(1), 47-59.

Torres, A. S. (2006). *Agent Based Models for integrated urban water management.* (P.hD). Retrieved from http://www. switchurbanwater.eu/outputs/pdfs/W1-2 GEN PHD D1.2.8 CWF Thesis Dissertation - Sanchez Torres.pdf

Tzima, F., Athanasiadis, I., & Mitkas, P. (2006). Report on the development of agent based models for water demand and supply. Nostrum-DSS. EC. http://www.feem-web.it/nostrum/ doc/d6-3.pdf

Van der Heijden, K. (1996). Scenarios: the art of strategic conversation.

Van Oort, F. (2002). Agglomeration, economic growth and innovation. *Spatial analysis of growth-and R&D externalities in the Netherlands.*

Vas, Z. (2009). Role of Proximity in Regional Clusters: Evidence from the Software Industry.

Von Hippel, E. (1976). The dominant role of users in the scientific instrument innovation process. *Research Policy, 5*(3), 212-239.

Wack, P. (2002). Uncharted waters ahead. *Strategy: critical perspectives on business and management. Vol. 2, 2,* 90.

Waldby, C. (2009). Singapore Biopolis: bare life in the city-state. *East Asian Science, Technology and Society, 3*(2-3), 367-383.

Wessner, C. W. (2009). *An assessment of the Small Business Innovation Research program at the Department of Defense*: National Academies Press.

White, R., & Engelen, G. (2000). High-resolution integrated modelling of the spatial dynamics of urban and regional systems. *Computers, Environment and Urban Systems, 24*(5), 383-400.

Wigand, R. T. (1988). High technology development in the Phoenix area: Taming the desert. *Creating the Technopolis. Ballinger, Cambridge (Massachusetts)*, 185-202.

Williams, J. C., ReVelle, C. S., & Levin, S. A. (2004). Using mathematical optimization models to design nature reserves. *Frontiers in Ecology and the Environment, 2*(2), 98-105.

Wong, K. W., & Bunnell, T. (2006). New economy'discourse and spaces in Singapore: a case study of one-north. *Environment and Planning A, 38*(1), 69.

Wooldridge, M., & Jennings, N. R. (1995). Intelligent agents: Theory and practice. *Knowledge engineering review, 10*(2), 115-152.

Wright, J., Kim, T., & Wiggins, L. (1989). *Expert systems: Applications to urban planning*: Springer-Verlag New York, Inc.

Yigitcanlar, T. (2009). Planning for knowledge-based urban development: global perspectives. *Journal of Knowledge Management, 13*(5), 228-242.

Yigitcanlar, T., Metaxiotis, K., & Carrillo, F. J. (2012). *Building prosperous knowledge cities: policies, plans and metrics*: Edward Elgar Publishing.

Yigitcanlar, T., O'Connor, K., & Westerman, C. (2008). The making of knowledge cities: Melbourne's knowledge-based urban development experience. *Cities, 25*(2), 63-72.

Yigitcanlar, T., & Velibeyoglu, K. (2008). Knowledge-based urban development: The local economic development path of Brisbane, Australia. *Local Economy, 23*(3), 195-207.

Yigitcanlar, T., Velibeyoglu, K., & Martinez-Fernandez, C. (2008). Rising knowledge cities: the role of urban knowledge precincts. *Journal of Knowledge Management, 12*(5), 8-20.

Yigitcanlar, T. A. (2007). The making of urban spaces for the knowledge economy: global practices.

Appendix-I

Brief Documentation regarding a series of Interviews with Senior principle planner of One north planning team (JTC) planner Mr. Andrew HO is given below.

1. How long was the design process- from start to end? How long is it approximately in other developments that you had visited? (Name few) what were the essential lessons learnt and implemented in one north?

    Ans. The masterplan concept development was an iterative process which took about 4-5 years to reach a 'steady-state'. The planning methodology was adjusted and refined based on the experience and feedback from pilot project implementations. The team visited projects in US, Europe, Japan, Korea, Hong Kong as well as reviewed literature on related projects. One of the key lessons learnt was the recognition of the fundamental importance of the implementation approach for the masterplan concept. A single-developer/controller model will have greatly different dynamics and issues compared to a multiple-developer/ controllers model.

2. What was your role and how many urban planners (Approx.) were involved in conceiving the masterplan?

    Ans. I headed the masterplan concept and development team. The team comprised 4-5 planners/architects but we worked in a multi-disciplinary environment with close interactions with the development and marketing team. The masterplan concept was developed through professional consultancy firms covering planning, engineering, transportation and a range of planning-related services.

3. What were some of the main goals in developing such a specialised environment for post- industrial cities? Do you think spaces such as one north could achieve them?

    Ans. To respond more effectively to a dynamic economic environment, to make better use of the resources to create a 'productive environment' which could stimulate growth of high-value activities.

4. What was the most difficult part of the planning and design process? Where did you feel less advice, as in could have had time or more clarity or academic help in general?

    Ans. Getting relevant inputs, and getting relevant stakeholders (including users) to try the new approach.

5. What aspect/activity/amenity do you think was missing in the design? (for e.g. housing, retail etc) what were the regulatory challenges? (e.g. URA, LTA, SLA, JTC)

    Ans. It's not so much what's "missing" in the design (from a planner's viewpoint), but how to get the critical functions and elements implemented.

6. There seems to be an underlying goal to increase the so- called knowledge interactions through physical design? How far did planners go as far as this is concerned?

    Ans. We had our plans for such 'interactions' but we are not able yet to measure /quantify the interactions, or success arising out of such interactions.

7. How much attention was paid to establishing the details of the actors and possible 'knowledge' interactions they might have?

    Ans. The one-north team was quite small – and given the huge complexity of designing a new approach and implementing it "on-the-fly", many issues could only be dealt with at a practical (tactical) level.

8. Did you think planners had sufficient information about what such interactions might possible be and how physical designs can be improved to achieve them?

    Ans. A key consideration is whether we are using a one-developer/ controller or multiple-developer/controllers approach. A second consideration is the available "levers" – the capability to control / dictate the developmental approach. It's difficult to identify and cover all parameters upfront in a masterplan.

9. What were some of the hurdles of identifying such interactions? How successful were planners in doing so given the time constraints? Who were consulted in such processes?

    Ans. Difficulties arise from the assumptions that planners have to make. For example, the hypothesis of one-north is that having a close-knit work-live-play-learn environment may give rise to more innovations through cross-interactions. However, finding the actual causation factors are very complex and difficult. Hence, one-north's approach is to build in a iterative process – "dynamic planning".

10. Do you think knowledge interactions between workers was a necessary part in the design process?

    Ans. Knowledge of how interactions works, the parameters creating /enabling such interactions to work – is definitely a key set of understanding to have for planners to build their frameworks.

Land Use Design Methodology

11. The word dynamic planning is used quite often in the masterplans, I reckon that spatially the plan with its vertical/horizontal integration is dynamic, in your opinion how does the land us design hold up temporally (over time)?

    Ans. In my opinion, "dynamic" and "planning" in this culture can be opposite forces. Land-use planning methodology in Singapore has largely remained the same over the last few decades.

    "Dynamic planning" was a term we used during the development of the one-north masterplan to refer to the need to respond in a timely manner to the changes in situation & environment. We observed that the conventional '2-dimensional' land-use planning could not respond effectively especially when there were un-foreseen outcomes. We wanted a balance between having a masterplan to oversee the development of the area, but we also needed additional 'levers' which could allow us to respond to new information / situation that arose - i.e to be able to make adjustments in timely manner, and preferably in a predictive manner rather than a reactive manner. Conventional land-use planning tend to remain rigid in between their review cycles.

12. Do you think a detailed zoning plan drawn up for 30 years was realistic? How useful are long term designs for postindustrial clusters with volatile demand characteristics?

    Ans. Long term detailed zoning plans are not flexible, but long term planning frameworks are necessary and important. There have been and will be many constraints in managing this "balance" between ensuring essential infrastructure is built in time, and flexibility to adjust in "micro-situations".

13. Apart from various social, economic and environmental goals mentioned in the masterplan, what were the instruments used by planners to facilitate knowledge interactions/spillover etc?

    Ans. Largely through focu groups and discussions with a broad range of stakeholders and partners. We also commissioned academic studies and worked with institutions.

14. I understand that, planners sought to develop a computer model for generating optimal design solutions, what was its purpose? IS it being used?

    A prototype software was developed but abandoned shortly afterwards. The cost factor was one inhibitor (the prototype model used commercially common software not suited for the intent). Another inhibitor was the 'fuzzy' brief given to the programmers at the initial stage (given the planning team at the start was also exploring around).

15. From the urban planning literature, I understand that master planning approach is static, un-responsive with a high obsolescence rate for dynamic spaces such as one north, in practice however is there an alternative methodology?

    Ans. *There are a range of alternatives – each with it's success and failures. Some seems to work better for its context, but not 'transplantable' – e.g Silicon Valley's innovation culture.*

    The approach we were experimenting in one-north focused on developing the masterplan as an overall guide, and incorporate flexibility in the detailed implementation plans. In otherwards, we adhered to the planning quantum parameters at the one-north district level, but allowed the various quantum to be re-distributed and transferred across sub-district levels - this way we hope to inject in flexibility in how the various usages can be combined for the desired outcome, and these optimal combinations can differ for different intended situations. Apart from the flexibility to redistribute /recombine usages at various sub-districts, it is also vital to have a information provision-and-feedback loop to allow planners to improve on their "solutions". Given that outcomes can take quite a while to be apparent, and feedback can get distorted going through multiple layers up the hierarchical command chain, hence it is important to develop the proper gathering and analysing systems to facilitate decision making.

Appendix-II

The Master plan phased development

As Figure 2.3 illustrates, the master plan followed by Singapore's 'One north' development consisted of creating three knowledge-specific zones. The first zone is a biomedical hub (Biopolis), followed by an engineering science complex (Fusionopolis) and a media and arts district (Mediapolis) – all of which are interspersed with housing, retail, commercial and recreational spaces. Each zone can be thought of as a district allocated with a dozen or more land parcels set to be developed independently over the course of the project.

The Biopolis

In 2003, the 'Biopolis' was the first development at One north Knowledge-Based Urban Development (KBUD), a new hub with high-profile space for biomedical research in Singapore. The development, standing adjacent to the research-intensive National University of Singapore (NUS) and the National University Hospital (NUH), hosts key biomedical public institutes together with local and global partnerships and forms the third node of a Biomedical Knowledge Corridor in Singapore (Waldby, 2009).

Some of the key public institutions located here are the *Institute of Bioengineering & Nanotechnology (IBN)*, the *Genome Institute of Singapore, Bio-processing Technology Institute (BTI)* and *Institute of Molecular* and *Cell Biology* (IMCB). Simultaneously, the Singapore Government allocated S$ 2 billion dollars for life sciences research in the year 2000, three years before the completion of the Biopolis at One north. This was followed by a S$5 billion dollar push for Science and Technology research in 2007 through the Biomedical Research Council (BMRC), a venture capital arm of the Science and Technology public policy organisation – A*star (Agency for Science and Technology).

To be developed in three phases over 15–20 years, the Biopolis at One North incorporates a slow-paced development strategy. The Biopolis first phase allowed for the development of the dynamic core of One north itself, creating a platform for the roll-out of phases II and III. This slow-paced development was a financially prudent measure to ensure that such a strategic development's feasibility is achieved before embarking on the next phase.

The development strategy of the *Biopolis* was to create distinct, yet complementary spatial facilities to enable the provision of an intellectually stimulating and creative physical environment for entrepreneurs, scientists and researchers to congregate and interact within different phases of the project. The phase I of the Biopolis at One north basically revolves around a large 1,85,000 sq m research complex, accommodating key biomedical research institutes and companies. At the Biopolis, companies can take advantage of shared cutting-edge laboratory space and access to scientific infrastructure to cut down R&D costs significantly and accelerate the development timeline. Flexible laboratory space sizes ranging from 219 to 1,100 sq m were planned to cater to diverse spatial needs of small and large organisations.

Figure 5.22 Illustration of the Biopolis master plan with predominant land uses

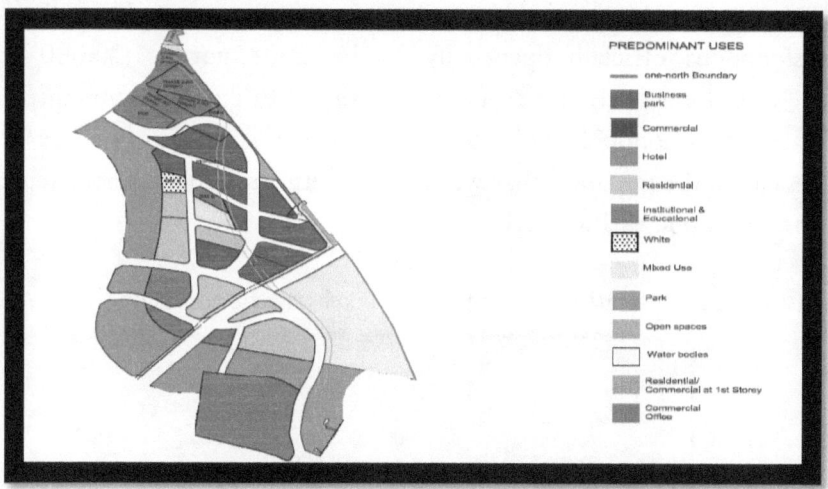

Source: (JTC, 2010)[13]

Office and commercial shop spaces with various floor plates are also catered in the facility in line with the mixed-use zoning nature of the development. By the end of 2012, Biopolis completed three phases of development successfully with a capacity to house around 6,500 workers (approximately).

Figure 5.23 Estimated space provided and number of workers in the Biopolis

Biopolis	Space provided	Number of workers (approximately)
Phase 1	1,85,000 m²	4,500
Phase 2	37,000 m²	1,000
Phase 3	41,505 m²	1,000

Source: Author's estimates (2013)

---

13 Truncated version of the Biopolis, from One north's master plan (see Figure 4).

Fusionopolis

Fusionpolis is the Physical Sciences and Engineering cluster spanning 30 hectares situated on the western part of One north. Phase 1 of Fusionopolis, officially opened in October 2008, covers 1,20,000 sq m (1.3 million sq ft) and costs S$600 million to develop. Subsequent phases of Fusionopolis will provide business and laboratory space to agencies and companies that will form synergistic collaborations with those from phases 1 and 2A.

Figure 5.24 Illustration of the phased development at Fusionopolis

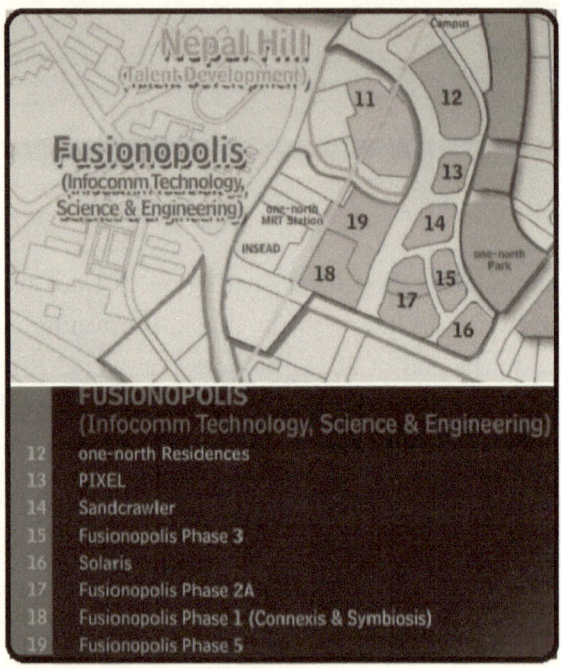

Source: One north masterplan, JTC (2010)

The Fusionopolis phase 1 development (Figure 8) consists of three towers (Connexis South, Connexis North and Symbiosis), with a gross floor area totalling 1,20,000 m². The first part of Phase 2B (Solaris), was completed in early 2010 providing over hundred thousand square metres of space for R&D in the Infocommunications, Media, Science and Engineering R&D industries at an estimated cost of S$148 million dollars[lxvi].

Figure 5.25 Estimated space provision at Fusionopolis

Fusionopolis	Space provided	Number of workers (approximately)
Phase 1	120,000 m²	4,500
Phase 2A	84,000 m²	1,000
Phase 2B	103,635 m²	1,000

Source: Author's estimates (2013)

Phase 2A is currently under construction and is expected to be ready in 2014, is a planned mixed-use development consisting of two towers hosting business parks, wet/dry laboratories along with office space on a 1.04 hectare piece of land with an approximate gross floor area of 84,000 (JTC official website, 2013).

Mediapolis
In year 2007, Singapore's media industry employed over 59,000 people, generated about 20.8 billion in revenue and created 5.1 billion in value added to the economy. The Singapore Government in 2009 infused S$230 million over the next 5 years to stimulate this sector for rapid expansion (Singapore Media Fusion, 2013[lxvii]).

Projected as Singapore's vital piece of media ecosystem, Mediapolis is a part of that vision- Mediapolis, a 19-hectare development within One north consisting of soundstages, digital production and broadcasting, green screen capabilities, Interactive Digital Media (IDM) and research and development activities interspersed with supporting amenities (retail, commercial, leisure, etc.) and housing (EDB, 2013). The development is a planned sub-cluster at One north, which is ready for a phased development for the next 15–20 years to push Singapore into a global media city by 2025. According the EDB, the rationale of such a venture would be to create and promote a 'cluster effect' for attracting new companies to set up their premises inside One north.

Figure 5.26 Estimated space provision at Mediapolis

Mediapolis (till 2012)	Space provided	Number of workers (approximately)
Phase 1	120,000 m²	4,500
Phase 2A	84,000 m²	1,000

Source: Author's estimates (2013)

The first phase of Mediapolis was launched in 2010 with the completion of the soundstage facility spanning 1.2 hectares, which would host the national media broadcasting company Mediacorp.

Figure 5.27 Demarcation of the Mediapolis sub-cluster at One north

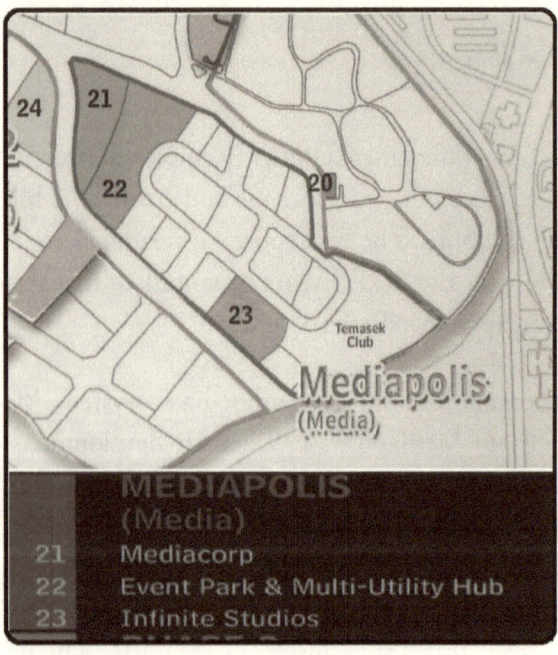

Source: One north masterplan, JTC (2010)

This is consistent with JTC's approach with other sub-clusters, where One north's initial anchor tenants are always from the public sector. This is to provide the necessary infrastructure, assurance and invitation for private companies to invest in the future of One north.

Wessex estate

The tranquil ambience of the south-western part of 'One north' consists of a long stretch of lush greenery providing housing for residents of the Knowledge-Based Urban Development (KBUD). Creating a dense housing mixture for knowledge-based workers that enhances cross-fertilisation of ideas seems to be an underlying goal. For this reason, priority is given to workers employed in any of the other three clusters (Biomedical, Physical sciences and Engineering and Media & Infocomm technology) within the development.

Figure 5.28 Typical housing type at Wessex estate, One north (Singapore)

Source: JTC website, 2012

The estate consists of 28 blocks of walk-up apartments (see Figure 15 (a)) and 58 semi-detached houses as shown in Figure 15 (b). Jurong Town Corporation (JTC), the industrial master planner of One north *"envisioned [Wessex estate] as a place where the gathering of diverse and creative minds will engender a bohemian culture that transcends norms and boundaries"*. The need for such a tranquil atmosphere for knowledge-based workers is based on the idea that some of the greatest innovations occur when people are exposed to natural habitats that help sharpen their thought process. Moving away from the bustling city life in theory seems to be supporting an environment conducive for innovation.

Appendix-III

HAT (Heterogeneity, Adaptability, Tractability) Framework
The 'Hetrogeneity, Adaptability and Tractablity' (HAT) framework broadly provides the necessary requirements to construct and benchmark an Agent Based-Land Use Model (AGB-LUM) to produce tractable scenarios of the Knowledge-Based Urban Developments (KBUDs). The 'Hetrogeneity, Adaptability and Tractablity' (HAT) framework was proposed by Arika Ligmann-Zielinska and Piotr Jankowski (2007) in their paper, which examines a generic robust framework for developing reliable agent-based models. The benchmark simply reflects one vision of a good, operational planning support model that balances scientific rigor and practical manipulability (Couclelis, 2002). It by no means represents the only plausible framework. The various components of the conceptual 'Hetrogeneity, Adaptability and Tractablity' (HAT) model framework are provided in Figure 4.1.

Heterogeneity is a key characteristic of Complex Adaptive Systems (CAS) that are often modelled with Agent-Based Modelling Systems (ABMS) (Benenson & Torrens, 2004; Bernard, 2002). In the agent-based models and as the different types of agents are introduced to represent multiple interests, the diversified actors such as the multiple developers, residents/tenants are defined.

Figure 5.29 Conceptual Representation of The Hetrogeneity, Adaptability And Tractablity (HAT) Framework

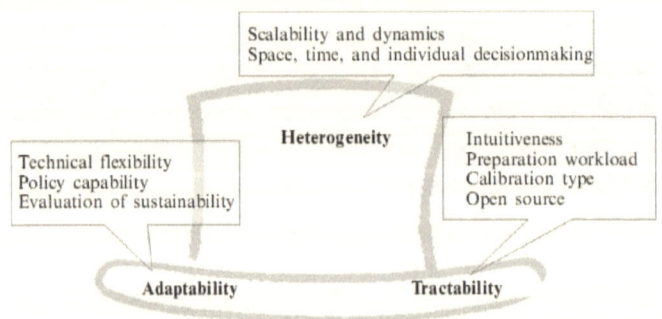

Source: Figure adopted and modified from Ligmann-Zielinska and Jankowski (2007); Author 2021.

Heterogeneity can also be introduced into the system under study through the following:

1) Differential time steps.
2) Spatial (environment) variability.
3) Dynamic hierarchies of system actors (e.g. the different types of organizations or family structures).

While urban modelling inevitably entails the consideration of explicit spatial variables (*Berger et al, 2002a*), previous land-use design models have been incapable of three-dimensional representation and manipulation (Wright, Kim, & Wiggins, 1989). The 'Heterogeneity, Adaptability and Tractability' (HAT) framework requires the Agent-Based Modelling Systems (AGMS) models to include four spatial scalability components, namely,

(i) model abstraction, that is, the vector.

(ii) representation, that is, the spatial and tabular input datasets to be included in the model (e.g. land use, zoning, vegetation).

(iii) resolution, that is, the smallest homogeneous spatial unit of analysis.

(iv) extent, covering the geographical location analyzed.

The last component of the heterogeneity arm of the 'Heterogeneity, Adaptability and Tractability' (HAT) framework is the notion of the agency in setting up an Agent-Based Modelling Systems (AGMS). Agency represents a counterpart of a real-world actor, be it animate (householder, developer, bird) or inanimate (car, house, business). If the model is set up to include different types of individuals (e.g. as owners, renters) but ignores the higher-level social structures such as families, then we are dealing with only the horizontal variety (weak agency) as opposed to the vertical variety (strong agency). When the model includes the social hierarchy (Benenson & Torrens, 2004) such as the parent agents and the child agents, who build family agents over time, then we have a strong agency. This agent scalability reflects the roles played by individuals in shaping the urban environment. The agent-based models often include interactive agents with a simplified internal structure that is adequate for the characterization of qualitative changes in spatial patterns. In summary, the agent-based model heterogeneity needs to consist of three dimensions, namely, time, space and human decision-making (DS function) as defined by Agarwal, Green, Grove, Evans, and Schweik (2002).

Adaptability refers to the ability of the model to allow for adjustments to the specific needs of geographic place, the problem to be resolved and the planning and design analysis phase. The 'Heterogeneity, Adaptability and Tractability' (HAT) framework's adaptability arm consists of the assessment indicators such as technical flexibility, policy capability and the evaluation of sustainability. A flexible Agent-Based Modelling Systems (ABMS) model should possess an easy interface with other models for the economic, environmental and impact analysis. The level of software in coupling with other formats such as the standardized GIS/AutoCAD output file formats, should be possible for useful examination (Boyd & Chan, 2002).

For the model to be useful for practical purposes, the modeller may include the diversity of policy variables. One can follow the policy categorization of land-use models by (Meyer & Miller, 2001) in which the policy variables can be divided into five categories, depending on their purpose. These categories are as follows:

1) Pricing
2) Regulatory
3) Infrastructure and services
4) Education
5) Marketing.

These help bring about community awareness through participatory urban planning (Burke, 1979). The sustainability of the development can be evaluated along with environmental criteria (conservation, green plot ratio and energy consumption), economic criteria (profitability) and social criteria (social equity and individual satisfaction) over the long term. However, a Land-Use Design model (LUDM) as the one proposed in this thesis (the Knowledge-Based Urban Development-Land Use Design Model (KBUD-LUDM) is incapable of assessing social and economic sustainability.

Model *tractability* represents the third arm of the Heterogeneity, Adaptability and Tractability (HAT) framework. This simply reveals information about the model's internal mechanics (mathematical formulations) that is both necessary for and represented in an understanable or intepretable format to the end user (model intuitiveness). The preparation overload may insist on explaining the database needs, both spatial and tabular formats, along with the programming effort involved in developing the Agent-Based Modelling Systems (AGMS) model (Anderson, 2002). The Agent-Based Modelling Systems (AGMS) can be calibrated using numerical variables (population, jobs, etc.), spatial data sets (land-use design zonal maps, GIS) or using block models (3D modelling), and so on. The final model validation takes place in legitimising the behavioural rules that drive the simulation process, which eventually has a critical impact on the overall model's output reliability (Benenson & Torrens, 2004).

Figure 5.30 Tabular representation of the Heterogeneity, Adaptability and Tractability (HAT) framework

---

Criteria for the HAT agent-based modelling and simulation assessment benchmarks

---

Heterogeneity

| Time | Scalability: duration and step |
| Space | Abstraction, representation, resolution and hierarchical variety |

Adaptability

Technical flexibility	Easy integration with other modules (economic, environment assessments and GIS coupling); output convertibility and case study adaptability [range-of-model-fit]
Policy capability	Pricing; infrastructure and services; regulatory; education/marketing

Tractability

Intuitiveness	Understandable model (transparent internal mechanics), mathematically tractable (verification)
Preparation workload	Dataset availability and extensiveness
Calibration (validation)	Numerical; spatial; behavioural and time
Open source	Algorithms – verifiable and shareable

Source: Adapted version of HAT framework proposed by Ligmann-Zielinska and Jankowski (2007)

The following are an extension of Section 4.2.

Secondary Agents

The above-given discussion regarding agent behavior and the optimization procedure is restricted to the primary agents, that is, the agents that are the main or anchor tenants of the Knowledge-Based Urban Developments (KBUD). However, for the supporting actors (e.g. retail, commercial, recreational and public spaces), their land uses also play an important role in facilitating a sustainable cluster. In our model, the secondary agents act as supporting actors to the anchor tenants and these are the additional land uses that the planner would wish to incorporate into the land-use design process. As secondary agents are complementary to the primary counterparts, they are often specified as ratios of the former. Planning and design questions relating to how much retail/commercial/recreational/green space should be allotted per person/per hectare/per person within a certain radius (meters) fall into this category.

To perform this task and in the land-use design agent-based model, the secondary agents follow three simple rules that are set out on a loop, up until the design is optimised for the primary agents in the model (step 5 in Table 10). In their first step, secondary agents are simultaneously created as soon as the primary agents for occupation are declared in the AIP (agent initialization procedure) procedure. Once the primary agents self-locate into land units, secondary agents follow and locate on or the nearest land unit from the primary agent of interest. The users may alternatively set a minimum of x percent gross floor area (GFA) for secondary units in each land unit to allow the secondary agents to support primary agents in every land unit. For example, one can cap retail (food and beverages) space in land units at 10% to allow for mixed-use (vertical) environments. Similar caps on land units may allow for other supporting land uses (residential, recreational, etc.) within the work environment.

Planners would also have urban design goals that stipulate the minimum amount of green space per person, the minimum amount of square foot of the built environment, the minimum amount of retail/commercial/ retail spaces to service the resident population, all of which have to be incorporated in the design process. Residential activity also becomes a major aspect of mixed-use developments and the supporting or service ratios are one way of providing adequate space for such infrastructure. In the 'One north' case study's initial design conception, these requirements existed throughout the master planning process. For such purposes, in my model I follow some of the important/necessary planning ratios deployed in the 'One north' Master Plan to be consistent with our case study used for subsequent empirical evaluation. For purposes of simplicity, the secondary agents (i.e. green space, commercial/retail, recreational and housing) are initialised with the following set of minimum requirements. The following minimum planning and data requirement are provided in Table 5.31 and it was used in the One north's design guidelines. I have used the same in the Knowledge-Based Urban Development-Land Use Design Model (KBUD-LUDM) for the 'One north' case study to facilitate the design standardization purposes.

In Table 5.31, the first column shows the housing type of secondary agents, while the second column more specifically states the planning ratios that are to be used in the Knowledge-Based Urban Development-Land Use Design Model (KBUD-LUDM). These figures are similar to the planning ratios deployed in the 'One north' Master Plan (JTC, 2010), See Table 5.2 in Chapter 5 for calculations.

Figure 5.31 Planning ratio assigned for housing in the Knowledge-Based Urban Development-Land Use Design Simulation Model (KBUD-LUDSM)

Type	Planning ratio	Distance
Housing Condominiums Semi-detached Detached	Service only 30% of total resident workers 1:3 (one unit for every three residents) 1:12 (one unit for every twelve residents) 1:6 (one unit for every six residents)	Nearest

Source: Adapted from 'One North's' Design Guidelines (JTC, 2010)

The third column specifies the minimum distance that the agents should be located from the primary agents that they service in the development. At each instance, the secondary agents servicing their primary agents would direct themselves into the nearest land unit with a specific radius that corresponds to its type of service. In the Knowledge-Based Urban Development-Land Use Design Model (KBUD-LUDM), each retail/ commercial or recreational space provided would be nearest from the central position of the primary agent that they are servicing. Previously, I had also mentioned agent allocation process for secondary agents that are not random. Owing to cost considerations, each type of activity has only a finite number of land units that they can use to service the primary agents. The interaction of these two constraints will be an important feature that would give some interesting results. Figure 5.32 illustrates and summarizes the entire land-use design simulation process and the model starts by adopting the agent initialisation procedure (AIP).

Figure 5.32 Land-use canvas represented by well-defined Polylines using Anylogic® Simulation Program for the case of 'One north'

Source: JTC (2010)

Figure 5.33 Detailed land use plan for the One north Baseline scenario (Chapter 6, Section 6.3.1)

Land Parcel Name	primary Agents	Type of Organisations				Retail	Housing	Total GFA required (sq m)	Footprint (sq m)	Floor Area Ratio (FAR)
		Tech firm (1.1)	University (1.2)	Research institutes (1.3)	Service firms (1.4)					
Biopolis										
BM_3	107	31	11	52	13	27		14,366	2,408	6.00
BM_4	0	.	.	.	.	.	200	2,415	2,318	1.00
BM_5	0	.	.	.	.	.	180	2,174	3,779	0.60
BM_6	92	28	5	50	9	33		12,517	2,036	6.10
Centros	92	37	6	42	7	58		12,527	2,048	6.10
Chromos	73	23	6	36	8	21		9,859	1,646	6.00
Nanos	104	36	11	48	9	18		14,021	2,137	6.60
Genome	76	24	9	37	6	2		10,229	1,692	6.00
Helios	181	55	20	92	14	11		24,407	4,014	6.10
Matrix	115	41	10	56	8	45		15,603	2,553	6.10
Proteos	160	64	12	73	11	.		21,758	3,973	5.50
Total (Biopolis)	1000	339	90	486	85	195	380	142,292	.	.
Fusionopolis										
CX3-6 (Fusionopolis)	751	234	75	575	67	56		101,326	9,274	10.90
CX3-4	255	71	24	130	30	15		34,311	7,507	4.60
CX3-1	0	.	.	.	.	.	500	3,625	4,315	1.10
CX3-3	.	.	.	.	.	.	150	1,328	1,702	1.06
Total (Fusionopolis)	1006	305	99	505	97	71	410	138,423	.	.

Source: Author, 2013

Note: Standard setback assumptions are 10% for industrial and 30% of total land for residential land uses.

Figure 5.34 5Illustration of the cost array table for 'One north' adopted for Knowledge-Based Urban Development-Land Use Design Model (KBUD-LUDM)'s agent environment*

Land parcels	Kb	Area (sq m)	Land use zoning (JTC)	Primary agent access	Development status	Max PR	Conservation status	Green space	Mixed use status	Retail	Residential status
Bm_7	A	4,054	Housing	0	1	4.00	0	0	0	0	1
P 1	A	1,693	PARK	0	1	1.00	0	1	0	0	0
OT-5	Sym	1,800	0	1	1	2.00	0	0	0	0	0
Chromos	A	1,828	B park	1	1	4.65	0	0	1	0	0
Genome	A	1,880	B park	1	1	4.65	0	0	1	0	0
P 2	A	2,131	PARK	0	1	1.00	0	1	0	0	0
E_6	A	2,220	Inst	1	1	2.90	0	0	0	0	0
Centros	A	2,275	B park	1	1	4.65	0	0	0	0	0
Nanos	A	2,374	B park	1	1	4.65	0	0	1	0	0
W11	Sym	2,662		0	1	4.00	0	0	0	0	0
CX4-7	Syn	2,676		0	1	6.00	0	0	1	0	1
S 1	Sym	2,735		0	1	4.00	0	1	0	0	1
BM_3	A	2,776	MU	1	1	5.30	0	0	0	0	0
CX4-2	Syn	2,821	0	1	1	9.00	0	0	0	0	0

Source: Land-use zoning data for 'One north', (JTC, 2010)
NB. A- *Analytica Kbase, Syn- Synthetic Kbase, Sym- Symbolic Kbase, B park- Business park, Inst-institutional.* *Complete data for all the 150 land parcels would be available on request.

Appendix-IV

The Validation procedure (continued)
The rise of models in the agent-based modelling (ABM) literature has led to an increased awareness among modellers to check and correct for path dependency and multiple equilibrium issues especially in economic, ecological and spatial land-use systems (Atkinson & Oleson, 1996; Balmann, 2001; Pahl-Wostl, 1995). Path dependency arises from negative and positive feedback that reinforce on each other to create large deviations from the optimal results. Thus, there is an increased necessity to validate spatial land-use models. Multiple equilibria is unfavourable as it increases model's uncertainty in obtaining land use design solutions for planning purposes. One can extend these concerns

to our model, which is a land-use design optimisation model. To get around this problem, D. G. Brown et al. (2005) suggest that modellers focus on two aspects to validate agent-based land-use models. The first is by employing *'aggregate similarity'* followed by *'spatial similarity'*.

Aggregate similarity is used to refer to similarities in statistical terms, whereby the mapped pattern of land-use design is in line with the functional relationships specified in the model. In other land-use agent-based models, this could be statistics that describe either the size of developed clusters, the relationship between distance to city centre, global density, or any other standardized performance measurements (Batty & Longley, 1994; Makse, Andrade, Batty, Havlin, & Stanley, 1998). The Knowledge-Based Urban Development-Land Use Design Model (KBUD-LUDM) for 'One north' generates optimised land-use designs for a given design criteria along with a set of rational assumptions (see Table 5.11). Thus, the *aggregate similarity* validation procedure would be able to test the robustness of the KBUD-LUDM's ability to generate optimal designs for varying inputs measured by the global parameters (∂_G & σ_G) for a variety of inputs and assumptions.

The performance of the global parameter Delta (∂_G)/Sigma (σ_G) obtained through the model using Eqs. (7) and (8) is used to evaluate the design outcomes for a given increasing set of agents and varying assumptions (see sets A–E in Figure 5.11 below).

This would act as a stress test to determine the robustness of the agent-based model to handle a variety of planning situations if the need arose. Table 5.9 shows the aggregate validation procedure performed for the Knowledge-Based Urban Development-Land Use Design Model (KBUD-LUDM) for the case study of 'One north'. Here, the first column (number of simulations) represents several rounds of stress tests using a set of initialization parameters and assumptions, which are given in Table 5.11.

Figure 5.35 List of varying assumption sets for the
empirical validation procedure for the KBUD-LUDM

Assumption Set	Number of agents	Agent characteristics		
		Knowledge base	Organisational	Institutional (Public-Private ratio)
A (Baseline)	2,000	$\alpha=0.5$, $\beta=0.5$, $\gamma=0$	$TF=0.30, RI=0.50$, $EI=0.10, SF=0.10$	80:20
B	3,000	$\alpha=0.3$, $\beta=0.4$, $\gamma=0.3$	$TF=0.10, RI=0.40$, $EI=0.20, SF=0.30$	70:30
C	4,000	$\alpha=0.2$, $\beta=0.3$, $\gamma=0.5$	$TF=0.60, RI=0.10$, $EI=0.10, SF=0.20$	60:40
D	5,000	$\alpha=0.35$, $\beta=0.1$, $\gamma=0.6$	$TF=0.10, RI=0.80$, $EI=0.05, SF=0.05$	40:60
E	6,000	$\alpha=0.1$, $\beta=0.8$, $\gamma=0.1$	$TF=0.15, RI=0.10$, $EI=0.10, SF=0.65$	20:80

Note: The agent's characteristics in Table 5.11 are assigned randomly
such that extreme values make a representative case to stress the model's
performance.

The second column of Table 5.9 shows the total number of agents
initialised, whereas the third column gives the output of the global
parameters – Delta (∂_G)/Sigma (σ_G) after the first round of simulation.
Results in Table 5.9 show the *aggregate* or empirical validation of
the Knowledge-Based Urban Development-Land Use Design Model
(KBUD-LUDM) developed for 'One north' Knowledge-Based Urban
Development (KBUD). The target for the global parameters (column

5) has been set with a twenty percent deviation window.[14] The optimal value for ∂_G is 0.5 according to the previously proposed knowledge interaction design criteria (KIDC) with a window of thirty percent standard deviation.

Column 7 in Table 5.9 tells us that the model for a set of assumptions (N), number of agents (x), at the nth simulation trial, whether the global parameter is satisfied or not. Iif the answer is a 'yes', then the Knowledge-Based Urban Development-Land Use Design Model (KBUD-LUDM) exports the design outcome as the final solution at every stage. To check for consistency of the results from the Knowledge-Based Urban Development-Land Use Design Model (KBUD-LUDM), the validation procedure can be performed for different combinations of 'actors' as shown inTable 5.9. A robust model should be able to deliver optimal solutions for different sets of agents and assumptions (Table 5.9).

The results do show that the KBUD-LUDM is able to handle multiple inputs and varying assumptions. For every set of assumption, the last column in Table 5.9 shows the solution of an optimum design at the nth trial where the global evaluation parameter delta's mean and deviation is considerably close to the optimal value. The optimal design solution for the last scenario (set E) however is unattainable. This was shown as an 'over stack' error with JAVA, i.e. one of the constraints adopted early on was too rigid.

---

14 As previously mentioned, the deviation window can be tightened or relaxed by the user. Ideally in a 'continuous' environment, this would not be necessary; however, in a constrained environment, optimal solutions are difficult to obtain. To get around this problem, I use a small deviation window. Theoretically, this does not challenge my design outcome as I previously claim the maximum interactive designs can be achieved within the 'optimal window'(∂) Figure 14, which leaves room for slight deviations from the norm.

Figure 5.36 Hypothetical example of the 'aggregate validation' procedure used for the Knowledge-Based Urban Development-Land Use Design Model (KBUD-LUDM)

Assumptions (as given in Table 5.10)	Number of agents	Cumulative agents in KBUD system	Global Delta (∂_G)	Target ∂ $\partial_G{\sim}0.50$	Standard deviation σ_G	Optimal design solution (Yes or NO)
Set A (baseline scenario)	2,000	2,000	$\partial_{TF}{=}0.70, \partial_{RI}{=}0.10$ $\partial_{EI}{=}0.10, \partial_{i}{=}0.10$	$\partial_G{=}.31$	0.26	Yes
Set B	3,000	5,000	$\partial_{TF}{=}0.70, \partial_{RI}{=}0.10$ $\partial_{EI}{=}0.10, \partial_{i}{=}0.10$	$\partial_G{=}0.43$	0.23	Yes
Set C	4,000	9,000	$\partial_{TF}{=}0.70, \partial_{RI}{=}0.10$ $\partial_{EI}{=}0.10, \partial_{i}{=}0.10$	$\partial_G{=}0.35$	0.22	Yes
Set D	5,000	14,000	$\partial_{TF}{=}0.70, \partial_{RI}{=}0.10$ $\partial_{EI}{=}0.10, \partial_{i}{=}0.10$	$\partial_G{\sim}0.59$	0.37	yes
Set E	6,000	20,000	$\partial_{TF}{=}0.70, \partial_{RI}{=}0.10$ $\partial_{EI}{=}0.10, \partial_{i}{=}0.10$	NA	NA	NO

Source: Author, 2013

The function of the cost-matrix is to restrict primary and secondary agents to specific land parcels to maintain development costs, n this case some of the secondary agents were found not to have space for allocation (refer to the cost-matrix given in Table 5.32). As secondary agents could not be satisfied, the loop was terminated resulting in an error. However, this is not to suggest that the framework is inefficient, but rather our cost constraints for the One north case study is stringent. This may be corrected by changing the fundamental assumptions of the planning ratios or the cost matrix to favour more secondary agents in the environment by enabling a more generous zoning to those actors.

The second type of validation is *spatial similarity* advocated in the literature (D. G. Brown et al., 2005), which refers to the degree of match between existing land-use maps and those generated using single or multiple runs of the subject agent-based model. The validation would entail a direct comparison between land-use designs (existing vs generated). In my thesis, I employ a two-tier visual validation procedure – the first being two-dimensional simulated outputs generated using agent-based modelling (ABM). The two-dimensional model is extrapolated into the three-dimensional block models to conduct a visual inspection against the existing block structures at 'One north'. There are several advantages of having a three-dimensional arm to a land-use design model; they have been adequately highlighted in Section 4.4. The baseline validation procedure in Section 5.9 has already performed the spatial similarity validation procedure; hence, I will not repeat this exercise again in this section. The baseline scenario shows the three-dimensional block diagram output from CityCAD* from the Knowledge-Based Urban Development-Land Use Design Model (KBUD-LUDM) agent-based model. However, this is by no means fully comparable to the built environment at One north, because complete path dependency for validation is not realistically achievable by the Knowledge-Based Urban Development-Land Use Design Model (KBUD-LUDM) as it is not a predictive agent-based model.

In a predictive agent-based model, the modeler often needs to answer the following question, *'Can the model predict past behavior?'* In the Knowledge-Based Urban Development-Land Use Design Model (KBUD-LUDM) model, one can approximately replicate the physical mould of One north at every stage of development, but existing land-use design details (mixed-use ratios) are hard to replicate for two reasons. Firstly, in the Knowledge-Based Urban Development-Land Use Design Model (KBUD-LUDM), the physical molds (plot ratio, GFA, etc.) are achieved through the allocation of actors on-site using the scientific principle of the knowledge interaction design criteria (KIDC), which was not the case for the land-use design exhibited in the masterplans. Secondly, even if mixed-use design ratios could be replicated, tenant data regarding current mixed-use design ratio at One north is unavailable for purposes of comparison.

Nevertheless, the aim of this thesis is not to propose a land-use design model to replace existing master planning techniques, but to enhance it to provide a more detailed and targeted and most importantly incremental[15] land-use design planning approach for Knowledge-Based Urban Developments (KBUDs). Traditional urban planning through master planning techniques has a top-down approach, where the physical planning informs current levels of *activity* on-site. I would call this as a more 'hardware' approach to modern industrial development, wherein physical planning is thrust without consideration of the probable interrelationship between actors on Knowledge-Based Urban Development (KBUD) sites.

For large-scale post-industrial clusters such as One north, given a set of actors, the Knowledge-Based Urban Development-Land Use Design Model (KBUD-LUDM) will facilitate planners to first achieve the right 'software' to enhance intra-cluster interactions between related actors and then upon which determine the space required to facilitate them through mixed-use zoning ratios (physical planning). Overall, this section concludes the empirical or aggregate validation procedure as advocated by D. G. Brown et al. (2005) for agent-based land-use models. We find that the Knowledge-Based Urban Development-Land The land-use design model (ie. The KBUD-LUDM) can report effective detailed land-use design solutions for a variety of assumptions and input data sets.

---

15   Incremental planning could be thought of a slow approach to urban planning
     and design rather than a one-shot completely top-down approach. Incremental
     planning is thus a more flexible option especially for large-scale projects with
     high uncertainty levels (Batty et al., 2000).

Chapter 5

The Conclusion

Chapter 5 summarises the books related literature. contributions, results, findings and recommendations. Chapter 1 explores qualitatively and quantitatively the extent to which the fundamental structure and behaviour of the large-scale high-tech strategic industrial real estate development project, can be shaped in terms of the institutional and macroeconomic conditions. A conceptual model is proposed of how such a large-scale strategic high-tech direct real estate development project, is shaped for Singapore's Biopolis at One North. Macroeconomic and institutional strategies by the EDB (Economic Development Board) and A*STAR (Agency for Science, Technology & Research), are found to influence the human, industrial and intellectual capital components of the Biopolis at One North.

The JTC (Jurong Town Corporation) has instrumentalised the physical mould of the Biopolis at One North via JTC's master planning and urban design strategies. Such foregoing government agencies morph the fundamental investment value of the large-scale high-tech strategic

Biopolis at One North development project, because the project affects demand for dedicated and specialized biomedical space in the space market. All the corresponding impacts are captured in an investment analytical model, which empirically estimates the tangible financial impacts on the fundamental structure and behaviour of the large-scale high-tech strategic industrial real estate at the project level. From Figure 10, the investment analysis, adopting capital budgeting techniques, shows a positive net present value (NPV), and a high enough after-tax internal rate of return (ATMIRR), in which the expected returns exceed the required returns. The risk analysis via adopting copula functions affirms the relative impact (in probabilistic terms) of the various uncertain macroeconomic and financial variables, on the profitability of the large-scale high-tech strategic industrial real estate development project like the Biopolis at One North.

Chapter 1 affirms the case of the Biopolis at One North for Singapore, in which favourable and sustainable industrial real estate market outlooks, relevant macroeconomic institutional policies and industrial urban plans, do positively shape the fundamental structure and value of large-scale high-tech strategic industrial real estate. More importantly, the extent to which the foregoing institutional policies can be reasonably expected to yield favourable risk-return investment values for large-scale high-tech strategic industrial real estate development projects, has been rigorously examined to be highly plausible via empirical evidence. Chapter 1 should be of primary interest to private and public listed real estate developers and policy makers, in bettering their understanding of the risk-return framework of such unique, large-scale high-tech strategic industrial real estate development projects like Singapore's Biopolis at the One North knowledge-based urban development (KBUD).

Figure 10. Distribution Of ATIRR From Monte-Carlo Simulations (Involving 10,000 Iterations)

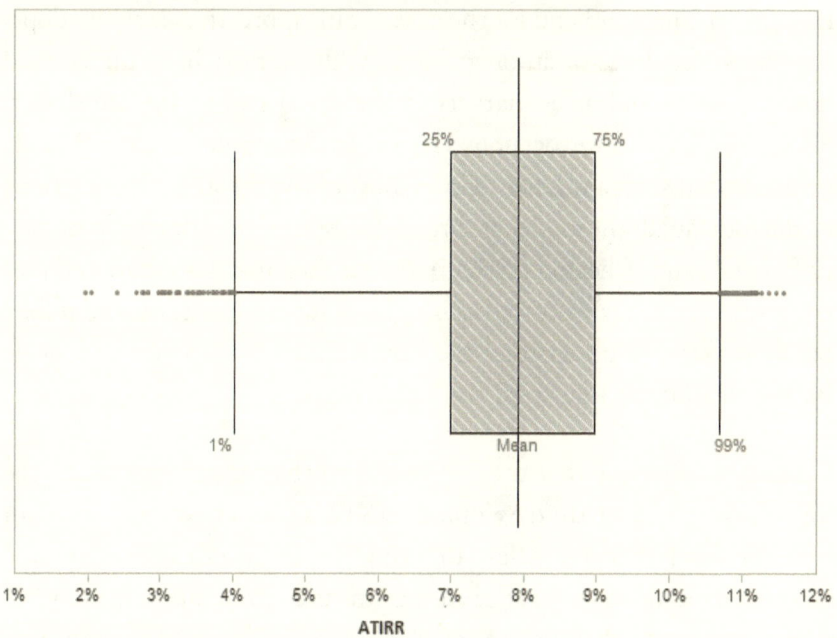

Source: Author, 2021

Chapter 2 looks at the related literature on the dynamics of the Strategic industrial real estate market with some notable exceptions (Kling & McCue, 2002; R. Thompson & Tsolacos, 2000; William C. Wheaton & Torto, 1990). Such notable exceptions are still scarce when compared to its counterparts like the housing and office sectors (Capozza *et al.*, 2002; Case & Shiller, 1989; Glaeser & Gyourko, 2006; Mankiw & Weil, 1989; Quigley, 1999). The aim of Chapter 2 to understand the fundamental structure and behaviour of the industrial real estate in Singapore, and to broadly indicate the relative impacts of macroeconomic conditions on real estate market dynamics. The Chapter acknowledges that the structure and function of Industrial real estate especially in developed economies are fundamentally changing, moving away from the traditional factory type model to more adaptable spaces that accommodate the creative and knowledge intensive industrial activities. These high-technology facilities have the potential to create more attractive and integrated workspaces that have high investment value. An understanding of their underlying factors is meaningful for academicians, investors and policy makers. In Chapter 3 and for the case of Singapore, the Chapter adopts the unrestricted vector autoregressive (VAR) approach, to understand how the space and asset markets in industrial real estate, are shaped via endogenous and exogenous factors. In Singapore, chapter 3 finds evidence that such a market follows most of the theoretical predictions of the four-quadrant model of direct real estate dynamics, proposed by DiPasquale and Wheaton (1999). The resulting model is robust and that the results are intuitive as well as insightful for academicians and public policy makers, to understand the behaviour of Singapore's large-scale high-tech strategic industrial real estate market.

Chapter 3 reiterates that the 21st century urban planners look to the knowledge-based urban development (KBUD) as a new form of urban renewal for industrial cities, to bring about sustainable economic prosperity and socio spatial order to the contemporary city.[lxviii] Inefficient large urban designs of planned post-industrial clusters have the undesirable outcome of creating the dissociation of related activities. Physical barriers can be on the rise that lead to a reduced level of intra cluster knowledge interactions via planned and spontaneous channels. Chapter 3 addresses the growing need for an urban design criterion that enables efficient land use planning for the KBUDs. Planned mixed-use land use designs can shape the knowledge interactions (KIs) between different types of actors by placing the 'related' workers together. A unique urban design criterion can be developed, aimed at enhancing the knowledge interactions (KIs) of the KBUDs.

Chapter 3 defines the KBUD 'actors' in terms of their specific roles in the KBUD innovation ecosystem. Drawing on the innovation and proximity dynamics literature, Chapter 3 proposes the knowledge interaction design criteria (KIDC) to enable urban planners to associate the related actors in space. With such a KIDC, the important rationale is satisfied when performing land use zoning 'to integrate compatible land uses, which generate positive externalities so that they are mutually beneficial (Chung, 1994)[lxvix]. The Chapter offers a formal representation of the knowledge based urban development-land use design model (KBUD-LUDM), incorporating the KI interaction design criteria, the KDIC via adopting agent-based modelling (ABM), to obtain the optimal land use design solutions. The contribution to urban planning and the KBUD design is twofold. First, Chapter 3 discusses how to identify and classify the complementary actors (i.e. the group) in a planned post-industrial KBUD. Secondly, Chapter 3 offers a dynamic alternative planning approach to 'zone' the KBUD via adopting the agent-based model, ABM.

Chapter 4 introduces that the ccity (urban) planners of the 21st century construe the knowledge-based urban development (KBUD) strategy, to be a new form of urban renewal of industrial cities. Many urban planners believe that such a new form of urban renewal potentially brings both economic prosperity and sustainable socio-spatial order, to the contemporary city[16]. From the field work interviews and surveys of the case of the One North knowledge-based urban development (KBUD), there first appears to be a general lack of understanding about the actors of the KBUDs. Then and to what extent can the diversity of the actors concerned favour intra-cluster interactions? Further studies should look into the determinants of interaction between actors and their reliance on space requirements to facilitate them. The result is that urban planners are compelled to explore 'interactive' environments, via physical planning (more specifically through mixed-use zoning), for the post-industrial cluster-based urban developments.

Long-term land-use planning and design are becoming a less favourable option among urban planners, owing to rising land and urban development markets' volatility. The outcome is demand fluctuations, which jeopardize existing mixed-use design ratios and complimentary zoning. Long-term traditional master planning is deemed to be simply too static for aiding the planning and development process of large-scale

---

16   See Lee et al, (2008), T. Yigitcanlar, Velibeyoglu, et al. (2008)).

dynamic KBUDs for the 21st century. Inefficient large-scale urban designs of planned post-industrial clusters have the potential to create the dissociation of related economic and physical activities over space. Such uninformed urban designs can increase physical barriers between 'related' actors. Consequently, there would be a reduced level of intra-cluster knowledge interactions via planned and spontaneous channels. There would be much less vibrancy for post-industrial spaces.

Several key questions can therefore be posed:

- Who are the actors of Knowledge-Based Urban Developments (KBUDs)?
- What is the theoretical urban design criterion that would maximize knowledge interaction among the participating actors?
- What is the optimal urban design of the Knowledge-Based Urban Development (KBUD), which enhances intra cluster knowledge interactions?
- How can we dynamically[17] design knowledge-based urban development (KBUD) systems?

The responses to the above questions are outlined herewith:

6. The actors of the KBUD comprise the primary and secondary agents. There are four generic actors, who participate in post-industrial clusters, namely, the technology firm (TF), the research institution (RI), the educational institution (EI) and finally the service firm (SF). Many post-industrial actors can be expressed as a combination of these primary agents. Secondary agents are supporting entities to the primary agents. The supporting activities can include the provision of green spaces, adequate housing, retail, commercial and recreational activities.

7. Well-planned mixed land use designs can help shape the knowledge-based interactions among the different types of actors. This

---

17 Or incrementally.

can be achieved by placing 'related' workers near each other via complimentary zoning. A unique urban design criterion is suggested, which seeks to enhance the KBUD's knowledge interactions (KI). Such a criterion can be used to identify 'related' actors if certain minimum information is available like the incoming participants in KBUD's. This criterion satisfies one of the three important rationales, adopted by urban planners when performing land-use zoning, to integrate compatible land uses, which generate positive externalities so that they are mutually beneficial. [18]

8. A knowledge interaction design criteria (KIDC) *is* proposed to obtain optimal land-use design solutions, via mixed-use zoning specifically for the KBUDs.

9. Agent-based modelling (ABM) is suggested as a dynamic methodology to handle spatial and temporal processes for land-use design optimization models, as compared to the simple and usual linear programming methodology that address land use design problems. A knowledge-based urban development-land use design model (KBUD-LUDM) is proposed that incorporate the knowledge interaction design criteria (KIDC). Such a model can be adopted for Singapore's One North KBUD, which demonstrates how urban planners can conduct incremental planning for long-term developments, like the KBUD via scenario planning and analysis.

10. Information and data on the environment and constraints for the KBUD-LUDM is sourced from the One North KBUD. The latter is an ideal case of the mixed-use development that aims to achieve intra-cluster interactions by accommodating a diversity of actors and activities. The agent-based model output produces two-dimensional land use maps an even three-dimensional block diagrams, via computer aided design (CAD).

---

18 The other two rationales are (2) separating incompatible uses that generate negative externalities and (3) interjecting public goods like roads and open space to improve social welfare (environmental benefits).

It is well known among urban planning professionals that long-term designs are too static to cater to dynamic environments like the KBUD. The inherent problem is the flight of labour and capital that the KBUD faces, owing to the forces of globalization. Rational planning models like the knowledge-based urban development-land use design model (KBUD-LUDM) can be extended to enhance its direct applicability to other case studies, apart from Singapore's One North KBUD. From Figure 4.15, the KBUD-LUDM adopts only two criteria, namely, the knowledge interaction design criteria (KIDC) and the land-use cost criteria (LUCC). To better integrate the two-dimensional and the three-dimensional outputs, the latest versions of the agent-based modelling (ABM) software program offer in-built three-dimensional modelling support. Therefore, there is no need to deploy any external computer-aided design (CAD) program. It may accordingly be well more efficient, be well saving on operational time, and to enhance the urban planner's engagement with the public at large, during the consultative planning process. Lastly, Chapter 5 concludes this book.

Figure 4.15. The Agent Based KBUD-LUDM, The KIDC & The LUCC

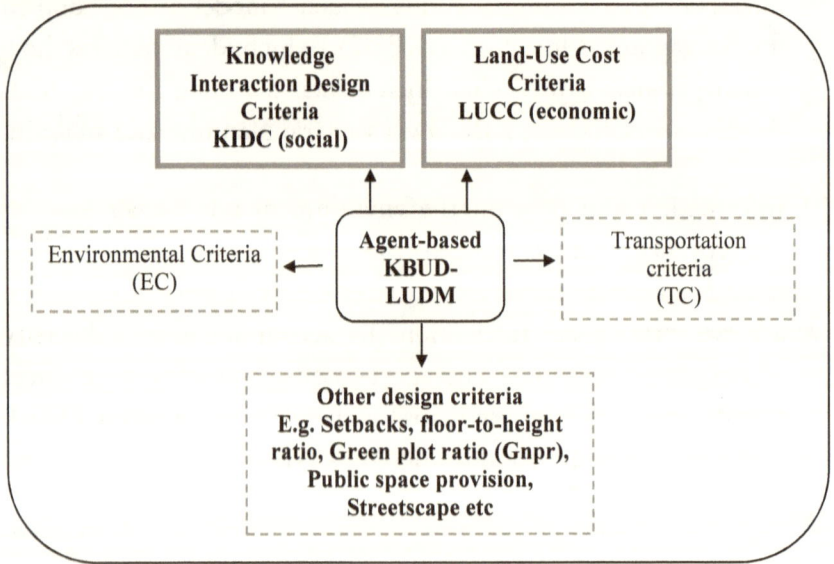

Source: Author, 2021

Endnotes

i   *The service industry today makes up about 69% share of nominal GDP making it the largest contributor. See Sing (2003). Source: MTI http://www.mti.gov.sg/ Pages/home.aspx*

ii   *Source: http://www.ura.gov.sg/interim/report1.pdf*

iii *Achieved by the state by land acquisition act (1966) see Zhu (2000).*

iv   *For more information on JTC's role in the industrial real estate market in Singapore, see sing(2003, p303)*

v   *http://www.a-star.edu.sg/portals/0/media/otherpubs/step2015_1jun.pdf*

vi   *Some of the industries that occupy such spaces are associated with R&D in fields such as information and communications (Info-Comm), biomedical/ pharmaceutical, engineering, media and the arts. See Zhu (2002), for an account of this changing physical landscape in Singapore.*

vii *One north is a planned knowledge-based development in Singapore that acts as a locus of industrial accommodation for knowledge intensive activities.*

viii *See, for a detailed account on the making of Biopolis in Singapore.*

ix   *We generalise the assumptions in order for the model to represent investment viability of similar hi-tech strategic industrial real estate.*

x

xi   *Phase 1, 2, and 3 have been completed and provides a total of over 278,500sqm of built-up space.*
     Phase 4 has been taken up by Procter & Gamble for its Singapore Innovation Centre.
     Phase 5 will provide 46,182sqm of biomedical research facility for additional laboratory space.
     Source: http://www.jtc.gov.sg/Industries/Biomedical/Biopolis/Pages/Biopolis.aspx

xii *Throughout Chapter 1 we are strictly referring to the Phase one of the Biopolis project that was launched in June, 2003.*

xiii *Truncated version of The Biopolis, from One north's overall master plan.*

xiv *Historical values were collected up to year 2011 to fit their respective distributions.*

xv   The Student3 (or 3-parameter Student) distribution is similar to the student-t distribution, but it allows for more flexibility as the mean can be different from zero and the standard deviation is specified as a parameter, and thus not dependent on the number of degrees of freedom (v) as in the case of a Student distribution. See (Vose, 2007).

xvi   ModelRisk risk analysis platform was used for all simulations.

xvii   It is important to note that as negative NPV does not equate to a loss, it means the value is below the cost of capital.

xviii   There is a very small chance (2.13%) of NPV being below zero.

xix   0-10% percentile comes to an operating expenditure of about ~ 20-22% using a Triangular fitted distribution.

xx   The 90-100% percentile comes to a OPE of about ~ 31-35% using the same distribution.

xxi   See Sing (2003).

xxii   Source: MTI http://www.mti.gov.sg/Pages/home.aspx

xxiii   Source: http://www.ura.gov.sg/interim/report1.pdf

xxiv   Achieved by the state by the land acquisition act (1966) see Zhu (2000).

xxv   For more information on JTC's role in the strategic industrial real estate market in Singapore, see sing(2003,p303)

xxvi   The reported depreciation rates for the U.S are around 2-3%.

xxvii   See Sing (2003).

xxviii Abeysinghe, T. (2007). Singapore: Economy Source: http://courses.nus.edu.sg/course/ecstabey/Singapore%20Economy-Tilak.pdf.

xxix   In 2010, of the total R&D expenditure (public & private) in Singapore Capital costs (land, building and machinery) made up 14.9% and manpower costs. We expect expansion of spending to generate demand for more high tech economic activity leading to demand of business and science park space.

xxx   Cap rate =NOI/C.V= (net operating income)/capital value where NOI= Annual rental yields minus maintenance costs+ miscellaneous income from property, we assume operating costs o be 10% flat for simplicity.

xxxi   For Singapore, the CLI includes the following time series, Total New Companies Formed Money Supply Stock Exchange of Singapore Indices, Business Expectations for Stock of Finished Goods (Manufacturing Sector) Business Expectations for Wholesale Trade, US Purchasing Managers' Index Manufacturing),Total Non-oil Sea Borne Cargo Handled, Domestic Liquidity Indicator (DLI) and Total Non-oil Retained Imports (NORI).

xxxii   Sing (2003) also addressed the short-run importance of interest rates in influencing supply in Singapore.

xxxiii See http://sbr.com.sg/commercial-property/news/chart-day-popularity-industrial-strata-titled-cushions-industrial-sector & http://www.colliers.com/en-gb/singapore/~/media/files/apac/singapore/research-reports/tp-sept2012-2.ashx

xxxiv

xxxv   *Data on annual R&D spending in Singapore was obtained from A*Star publications (2010).*

xxxvi   *We used WLS instead of OLS since the model's residuals exhibited non-constant variance in the sample.*

xxxvii *Granger causality tests results can be obtained on request.*

xxxviii *http://www.singstat.gov.sg/pubn/papers/economy/ssnsep07-pg1-6.pdf*

xxxix   *This is because cap rates are a ratio of net income from properties (rental yield minus operating expenditures) to capital value. So an increase in capital values will naturally bring the cap rates down keeping everything else constant.*

xl   *We can assume increases in the cap rate in the short term (one to three quarters) are mainly due to the more volatile rental yields, as in our sample property prices are more stable in the short run.*

xli   *Albeit with low Significance of 10%*

xlii   *Granger casualty tests show casualty running from PPI, VC to capitalization rates in Singapore and not the other way around (significance at 5% level).*

xliii   OECD (2000).

xliv   Storper (1992); Cesaroni and Piccaluga (2003).

xlv   With the exception of (Allen, 1984); Toker and Gray (2008).

xlvi   See for city branding.

xlvii   In Chapter 3, urban design criteria refer more specifically to the land-use design criteria that determine the spatial allocation of activities.

xlviii A characteristic feature of workers in knowledge-based industries.

xlix   Urban precinct here is defined as an election district of a city or town.

l   http://www.urbandesign.org/
        These interactions can be social (by aggregating residential land uses), economic (establishing business clusters), environmental (providing access to green space, conservation), and so on.

li

lii   http://www.urbandesign.gov.au/whatis/index.aspx

liii   Actors who belong to a common economic, institutional or organizational entity.

liv   An example of regional agglomeration would be the 'Blue Banana' in Western Europe. The financial centres in the city of London and advertising industry at 'Madison Avenue' in New York are good examples of industrial agglomeration on a metropolitan and neighborhood level.

lv   The word 'actor' here in this context is used to refer to knowledge workers who participate in knowledge-based clusters

lvi   See Asheim and Gertler (2005) for a detailed discussion.

lvii   This is equivalent to reducing the average geographical distance between actors in the Knowledge-Based Urban Development (KBUD).

lviii   Bounded rationality is the idea that in decision-making, rationality of individuals is limited by the information they have, the cognitive limitations of their minds, and the finite amount of time they must decide.

lix   Note: The organizational proximity refers to both inter-organization and intra-organizational proximity between agents.

lx   Apart from the most common subsidiary land uses, for a knowledge-based development this could be more specific amenities such as seminar rooms, libraries, cafes, restaurants, and so on.

lxi   Optimization is given in equation (3.1).

lxii   See Lee et al, (2008), Yigitcanlar, O'Connor, et al. (2008)

lxiii   While the other two rationales are (i) separating incompatible uses that generate negative externalities and (ii) interjecting public goods like roads and open space to improve social welfare (environmental benefits).

lxiv   http://www.a-star.edu.sg/Biopolis-Fusionopolis/A-Vision-for-Convergence/Fusionopolis.aspx

lxv   http://www.ascendas.com/images_common/cms/press_release/137/Press_release_-_First_Building_at_Mediapolis_11Feb2011.pdf

lxvi   http://www.jtc.gov.sg/Publications/Newsletter/Periscope/2008_05/news-perspectives/article02.htm

lxvii   http://www.smf.sg/Pages/SingaporeMediaFusion.aspx

lxviii   See Lee et al, (2008), Yigitcanlar, O'Connor, et al. (2008)

lxix   While the other two rationales are (i) separating incompatible uses that generate negative externalities and (ii) interjecting public goods like roads and open space to improve social welfare (environmental benefits).